'This book is going to change and save so many lives. It's a vital exploration into autism, gender and sexuality, and is easy to understand even as it tackles difficult topics. The intersectionality between autism and LGBTQIA+ identities has long been ignored, but *Queerly Autistic* not only bridges the gap but guides the reader through a world of new ideas and acceptance. A pleasure to read, and to be seen. One of the most important books in autistic literature.'

– *Poe Charlotte, author of* How to Be Autistic

'Erin's no nonsense, clear and concise explanations of the many roads that lead us to self-discovery re: gender and sexuality is carefully crafted. For any young autistic (or otherwise) person questioning the many variables to working our where you "sit" and how to recognise your "fit" within queer society, this book is perfect!'

– Dr. Wenn B. Lawson (PhD) CPsychol AFBPsS MAPS

'Ekins has created an essential guide for autistic LGBTQIA+ teenagers, covering all aspects of identity, relationships and, crucially, safety. Informative and refreshingly honest, Queerly Autistic provides a definitive and clear framework for LGBTQIA+ autistic teens navigating the highs and lows of life. Every LGBTQIA+ autistic teen needs a copy of this on their shelf.'

– *Lizzie Huxley-Jones, editor of* Stim: An Autistic Anthology

'A well-articulated and queerly presented book, written in an accessible way for people to enjoy and learn. Erin allows the reader to take their own path into understanding more about where their particular queerness and autism intersect. An important book, reminding us that our queer community is so wonderfully diverse and vibrant.'

– *Fox Fisher, artist, author and film maker*

'What a wonderful resource for people that exist on the intersection of being queer and autistic. It will undoubtedly help many people and affirm them, in a world that is constantly questioning them and their ability to make their own decisions. A brilliant book!'

– *Ugla Stefanía Kristjönudóttir Jónsdóttir (Owl), author and campaigner*

'As an autistic person who both got my autism diagnosis and came into my queerness later in life, it is hard to express the feeling of comfort there was in reading a book written for the confused queer autistic kid I was. It is also so important that Erin is an autistic author writing for autistic readers. This kind of knowledge exchange is so powerful and still far too rare.'

– Kate Sauder, disability scholar and blogger

'*Queerly Autistic – The Ultimate Guide for LGBTQIA+ Teens on the Spectrum* is such an important and much needed book. The clear, matter-of-fact way it deals with complex and sometimes difficult topics is so accessible and easy to understand, as are the suggested 'scripts', and signposting to further support. The repeated advice, using the same language for different topics, not only makes the book easy to dip into, but also makes the suggested guidance clear and easy to remember. For any LGBTQIA+ teen, and not only those who know they are autistic, this book could provide a life-line to understanding and making sense of their identity and crucially recognising they are not alone.

Erin shares her lived experiences of being "queerly autistic" in a way that will no doubt support and resonate with so many autistic young people. She is clear that, for example, when discussing difficulties some autistic people have in identifying and describing emotions... 'This doesn't mean that we aren't able to know or make decisions about our sexuality or our gender identity. Many of us simply need support and safety in order to properly understand ourselves and our feelings.'

This book might be the starting point a person needs to begin to feel that support and validation. Anyone who cares for or has responsibility for teenagers, whether autistic or not, should read it and learn from it to be able to better offer further safe support and understanding.

Whether you are a queerly autistic young person, or someone who knows, loves or supports one, Erin's empowering closing words are the reason you should read this book: Be proudly autistic, be proudly queer, and be proudly you.'

– Joe Butler, SEND Support (@SENDsupportuk)Education/Disability Consultancy and Training

'Such a kind and needed book!'

– Hannah Witton, author and broadcaster

QUEERLY
AUTISTIC

of related interest

Spectrums
Autistic Transgender People
in Their Own Words
Edited by Maxfield Sparrow
ISBN 978 1 78775 014 2
eISBN 978 1 78775 015 9

Gender Identity, Sexuality and Autism
Eva A. Mendes and Merideth R. Maroney
Foreword by Wenn Lawson
ISBN 978 1 78592 754 6
eISBN 978 1 78450 585 1

The Spectrum Girl's Survival Guide
How to Grow Up Awesome and Autistic
Siena Castellon
Illustrated by Rebecca Burgess
Foreword by Temple Grandin
ISBN 978 1 78775 183 5
eISBN 978 1 78775 184 2

The Autistic Trans Guide to Life
Yenn Purkis and Wenn Lawson
Foreword by Dr Emma Goodall
ISBN 978 1 78775 391 4
eISBN 978 1 78775 392 1

Gender Explorers
Our Stories of Growing Up Trans
and Changing the World
Juno Roche
Foreword by Susie Green
ISBN 978 1 78775 259 7
eISBN 978 1 78775 260 3

Queerly Autistic

The Ultimate Guide For LGBTQIA+
Teens on the Spectrum

Erin Ekins

Jessica Kingsley Publishers
London and Philadelphia

First published in Great Britain in 2021 by Jessica Kingsley Publishers
An Hachette Company

1

Copyright © Erin Ekins 2021

The information contained in this book is not intended to replace
the services of trained medical professionals or to be a substitute for
medical advice. You are advised to consult a doctor on any matters
relating to your health, and in particular on any matters that may
require diagnosis or medical attention.

Trigger Warning: This book mentions anxiety, bullying, homophobia,
rape, sexual abuse and transphobia.

A CIP catalogue record for this title is available from the British Library
and the Library of Congress

ISBN 978 1 78775 171 2
eISBN 978 1 78775 172 9

Printed and bound in Great Britain by TJ Books Ltd

Jessica Kingsley Publishers' policy is to use papers that are natural,
renewable and recyclable products and made from wood grown in
sustainable forests. The logging and manufacturing processes are
expected to conform to the environmental regulations
of the country of origin.

Jessica Kingsley Publishers
Carmelite House
50 Victoria Embankment
London EC4Y 0DZ

www.jkp.com

Contents

Acknowledgements

There are so many people without whom this book would never have happened. To take full credit for anything in these pages would be dishonest. I would not be where I am today without the ongoing emotional, physical and professional support of these people.

Firstly, to my fearsome beasts, Thor and Odin. This book wouldn't have been possible without the gentle warmth of you sitting on my feet until all circulation was cut off, nor without your gentle pathetic whines to try and get my attention as I rushed to meet a deadline. I've made it my life's mission to be as good a person as you ridiculous doggos think I am.

To my mum for always being my biggest cheerleader, even before my diagnosis when we didn't have a solid reason why I was finding life so hard. That my journey and pride with my sexuality was fundamental to your own coming out journey is the ultimate achievement in my life.

To the rest of my family – my stepmum, my brother, my dad – for always supporting me and having my back, even when I wasn't always the easiest person to be around. Researching and writing this book has hammered home to me that many people do not have people like you in their lives, and I am lucky.

To Fiona for putting up with me for the last decade - you are always ready to let me bounce a million ideas off you and always have a sensible word to put in when I'm falling apart. I would never have known I was autistic without you, and I genuinely believe you saved my life.

To my gorgeous Chryedians: Jenn, Alex, Jenni, Han, Mads, Steph and Kat, who always make me smile and didn't hold back when I sent you the first draft to pick apart. Thank you also for the long middle of the night discussions about fandom, shipping and its relationship to gender and sexuality.

To Jules and all the other Torchwood fans who were there when I was figuring out my sexuality, and who helped me get through the death of my first fictional bicon.

To Mav, for reading the first draft of this book so quickly and getting back with invaluable advice. You were always going to be the hardest person to please, and when you told me that you not only enjoyed the book, but wished you had had it growing up, that was truly the moment I believed this was actually a thing that might work.

To Andrew at Jessica Kingsley Publishers for taking a chance on me and giving me the opportunity to fulfil this dream. To Emily, Isabel, Emma and everyone else at JKP who has helped work me through the process of writing and publishing my first book.

To Owl and Fox Fisher, incredible trans activists, writers and filmmakers who have inspired me for years. If not for my last-minute decision to attend your book launch that day in 2018, I would never have met the crew at JKP and this book would still be but the seed of an idea.

To all the amazing writers and content creators whose works I have referenced in this book. You are changing the world and saving lives and you should be so, so proud of everything you do.

And to all the amazing autistic LGBTQIA+ folks out there, writing books, posting on social media, delivering talks, just living your lives in the most brilliant queerly autistic way. You are my everything.

The Double Rainbow

H ello there!
My name is Erin. On the internet, I am also known as QueerlyAutistic.

This is because I am queer. And I am autistic. I like to say that I live under the double rainbow.

But what is the double rainbow?

The LGBTQIA+ (lesbian, gay, bisexual, transgender, queer/questioning, intersex, asexual, and other non-straight, non-cisgender identities) community is represented by the rainbow flag. Designed by Gilbert Baker in 1978, at the request of famous gay politician Harvey Milk, the rainbow was a symbol for San Francisco Pride. It has since spread as a symbol for the LGBTQIA+ community across the world – the different colours of the rainbow capturing the different people and identities who live under it.

We also know that autism is described as a spectrum. I

was personally diagnosed with 'autism spectrum disorder'. Autistic people are often referred to as being 'on the spectrum'. This is because it's a wide range of behaviours and experiences grouped together. Not all autistic people have the same traits, but we often share similarities. The word 'spectrum', however, is also a scientific term, meaning the rainbow of colours in visible light.

This is why autistic LGBTQIA+ people are sometimes referred to as existing under the 'double rainbow'.

This term exists because of one reason: a greater percentage of the autistic population identifies as LGBTQIA+ than the non-autistic (neurotypical) population.

There have been a number of studies into this. Some of these studies have tried to get the figures on how many autistic people actually identify as 'not straight' or 'not cis'. Others have tried to compare the number of autistic people who identify as LGBTQIA+ against the number of neurotypical people who identify as LGBTQIA+. Many have focused on the crossover between being autistic and having a trans identity (as these numbers appear to be particularly high when compared with the neurotypical community). Further studies have tried to get to the bottom of the crossover between LGBTQIA+ and autism, to explain it in medical or psychological terms, and to try to answer the question: why?

In the process of doing research for this book, it has become painfully obvious to me that very few of these studies involved autistic LGBTQIA+ people in any real way. One study in particular attempted to draw a line between 'sexual identity' and 'sexual behaviour', pointing out that many autistic people studied 'claimed' to be LGBTQIA+ and yet had never had sex with someone of the same sex (implying that sexuality is based on your sexual history rather than your knowledge of your own attraction and identity). It also suggested that many autistic men may identify as 'non-heterosexual' simply because they were nervous about approaching girls.

Not only is this insulting to the many autistic LGBTQIA+ people out there (plus autistic people and LGBTQIA+ people individually), but it's not reflective of the reality that I have found as a person actively existing, socializing and advocating under the double rainbow. The unfortunate fact is that many of these studies simply fail to recognize that autistic LGBTQIA+ people are real people, living real and varied lives. More disappointingly, however, they never actually address the things that would have helped me as a young autistic LGBTQIA+ person.

That's why I decided to write this book.

As a teenager, I desperately needed something that could guide me through life as an autistic LGBTQIA+ person: through working out my identity, coming out to family, friends, colleagues and strangers, finding support, getting involved in the community, and safely navigating friendships and relationships as both autistic and LGBTQIA+.

I needed someone to hold my hand and tell me what to do, what to expect, and to reassure me that it was going to be okay. Or, at the very least, that it wasn't going to be quite the horror show I had created in my mind.

I came out as bisexual when I was 16. I started identifying as 'queer' as well as bisexual when I began getting involved in campaigning at university. I've always been a shouty person who wants to change the world for the better. Seeing injustice has always been physically painful for me.

As much as I worked towards being proud of my sexuality, I still found it difficult to find my place in the LGBTQIA+ world. I just couldn't find where I belonged. I still felt different, detached, as though everyone around me was tapping into something that I couldn't quite get a handle on.

Then, when I was 23, I got my answer: I am autistic as well.

This opened up a whole new door of possibilities for me. As comedian and writer Hannah Gadsby says, my diagnosis 'was like being handed the key to the city of me'.

For the first time, I understood myself fully. I also understood myself as a queer person fully, and why I had struggled to find my place in the queer world.

In some ways, I was lucky. By coming out years before my autism diagnosis, I had managed to avoid a lot of the denial around sexuality, gender and autism. Nobody ever questioned whether I could or should be queer, or even if I should have a sexuality. That kind of pushback was never a part of my coming out story.

But I always was autistic. I was autistic when I was figuring it out. I was autistic when I was coming out. I was autistic when I was building relationships for the first time. I was autistic when I tried to go out and about in the queer community. I was autistic while trying to deal with the bigotry and injustice that sometimes come part and parcel with living loudly as a queer person.

And a book like this would have helped make that process so much easier.

So I hope this is helpful to you. I hope that this is at least a small bit of guidance on the winding road that is figuring out who you are and who you love.

We're going to look at the whole spectrum of experiences that you might have as an autistic person figuring out and exploring your sexuality and gender. This will include:

- The definition and history of some of the labels people use for their sexuality and gender.
- What attraction feels like and ways to help you figure out your sexuality.
- What gender feels like and ways to help you figure out your gender identity.
- Coming out (telling people about your sexuality and gender) and how to be safe while doing it.
- What it means to undergo gender transition and the different journeys you can take to do it.
- Different types of relationships and how to navigate them (including how to spot, avoid and escape toxic or abusive relationships).
- Understanding consent and having sex safely as an LGBTQIA+ person.
- Being out and about in the LGBTQIA+ community and finding community spaces that work for you.
- How to deal with bullying and injustice, and ways you can make a difference.

Throughout the book, I'll be providing links to organizations, helplines, advice, support and information. Where there is a helpline, I have made sure to include different ways that you can make contact without making a phone call, as many of us struggle with this. This includes live chat options, email addresses and text options.

At the end of each chapter, there will be a short list of books, links and YouTube videos. These are the resources that I have used to help me in writing each chapter, and they might be helpful to you too. If you see a book appear in multiple chapters, it's because that book contains information related to all of those chapters: for example, if I recommend a book in the 'figuring out your sexuality' section and the 'relationships' section, it means there is useful stuff in that book on both of those topics.

Most of the YouTube videos I link to are channels run by LGBTQIA+ people, so you might want to explore more of their work aside from the videos I provide.

Remember, I don't have direct experience with all of the things I am writing about in this book. I had to do a lot of learning and a lot of listening in order to write it, and I'm certain there are things that I have missed. It's also worth remembering that I am a white woman, and that this book has been written through a white lens because of that. The experiences of the LGBTQIA+ community are as diverse as any other, and although I have tried my best, it's always a good idea to reach out for more information, more experiences and more conversations around sexuality and gender.

Instead of thinking of this as the ultimate source for all things queerly autistic, think of it as a primer at the start of a long and wonderful journey.

You don't have to be queer, trans or autistic in order to read this book. Although it was written with people like me and the people I love firmly in mind, I also wrote it as a primer on all things related to sexuality and gender. So, if you're not autistic, but you're struggling with your sexuality or gender, this book might be helpful. Or, if you know someone who is queer, trans or autistic, this book might give you an insight and understanding into what they're experiencing.

The topics in this book are things I think everybody should know about.

Being queerly autistic is brilliant, and complicated, and fabulous, and hard, and beautiful, and something that I would never ever change about myself now – even if, for some of my years, maybe I would have changed it, given the chance.

I never want you to be where I have been. You deserve better than that.

So whether you *know* that you live under the double rainbow, or you're just peeping around the corner and sussing out whether you should move in, or you just want to find out more about this particular rainbow in all its glory, then this book is for you.

CHAPTER 1

What is LGBTQIA+?

As we'll be using the phrase 'LGBTQIA+' throughout this book, it's important to talk about what it actually means.

The term you are most likely to hear people use is 'LGBT'. This is a commonly used acronym that stands for lesbian, gay, bisexual and transgender. You may also hear people say:

- LGBT+
- LGBTQ
- LGBTQ+
- LGBTQIA
- LGBTQIA+
- LGBTQIAP
- LGBTQIAP+
- Queer
- MOGAI (marginalized orientations, gender alignments and intersex)

As you can see, different people have different names for the same thing. This is because it covers a huge array of different people, identities, and experiences.

And while some people (including many charities and news outlets) may use 'LGBT' for brevity, many others will use 'LGBTQIA+' in order to include as many people as possible. In this book, we will be using the term LGBTQIA+. This is because it is concise, recognizable and includes (celebrates) a wide variety of different people that exist in the community (although still not all).

In this chapter, we're going to have a look at some of the different identities included under the LGBTQIA+ umbrella. We're going to have a look at what the terms mean, the history behind them, and some famous people who use these identities. There will also be a few words from autistic people who use those identities and what it means to them.

For autistic people, labels and definitions can be incredibly helpful when it comes to figuring things out. For example, when I was learning to drive, I could only work out how to change gears after I knew every little detail of what was happening when I moved the gear stick, what the mechanics were, and why they did what they did. It's how we make sense of the world.

Of course, there's more to figuring yourself out than labels alone (as we will see in the next chapter), but it's a very good place to start.

Lesbian

A lesbian is a woman, either cis or trans (you can find out what these mean in the 'transgender' section of this chapter) who is sexually and romantically attracted to other women (both cis and trans). Some women prefer to call themselves gay, so it's important to try and use the language that a person is comfortable with.

The word 'lesbian' originally referred to residents of the Greek island of Lesbos. At some point in the last 150 years, it started being used to describe 'women who love women'. This is because the island of Lesbos was home to the Ancient Greek poet Sappho, who wrote poems proclaiming her love for other women. This is also why you may sometimes hear lesbians or gay women refer to themselves and their relationships as 'sapphic'. The term lesbian was originally used to describe any woman who had sexual or romantic relationships with other women (including women we would now call 'bisexual'), but is now most commonly used to describe women who have sexual and romantic feelings for other women exclusively (although this isn't true for everybody who identifies as a lesbian).

You may also sometimes hear the term 'gold star lesbian' to describe a woman who has only ever had romantic or sexual relationships with other women. Please don't take this to heart if you are a lesbian who has had relationships with men. No lesbian is a 'better' lesbian than any other. Some lesbians have previously had romantic or sexual relationships with men, and some lesbians have never had a romantic or sexual relationship with a man. Either way, they are still lesbians, and they are still valid.

Here are some people you may have heard of who identify as lesbians:

Hannah Gadsby: an autistic comedian and writer who has two comedy shows on Netflix (*Nanette* and *Douglas*). She received a late autism diagnosis and has spoken openly in her comedy about her sexuality and her autism.

Lena Waithe: a screenwriter, producer and actress who has starred in *Master of None* and *Westworld*. She said at the Essence Black Women in Hollywood Awards 2018: 'Being born gay, black and female is not a revolutionary act. Being proud to be a gay, black female is.'

Jessica Kellgren-Fozard: a British YouTuber who is openly lesbian, disabled and deaf. She makes content about being her love of vintage fashion, her experiences being deaf, issues facing the disabled community, LGBTQIA+ history, and the intersection of being LGBTQIA+ and disabled. She has been featured in the media and on broadcast television talking about disability and LGBTQIA+ issues. She is married and her wife, Claudia, often appears in her videos.

Gay

Although 'gay' is used to refer to all people who have exclusive same-gender attraction, we will be focusing on gay men in this section.

A gay man is a man, either cis or trans, who is sexually and romantically attracted to other men (both cis and trans). As we said in the previous section, some women prefer to call themselves gay rather than lesbian, but most gay men prefer to use the term 'gay'.

Originally meaning 'joyful' or 'carefree', and then evolving to mean 'debauched' or 'pleasure-seeking', in the last 100 years the word 'gay' has evolved to mean 'homosexual'. As the term 'homosexual' has fallen out of favour (due to it being a medical term used at a time when it was seen as an illness), 'gay' has become the most commonly used word to describe people, particularly men, who are sexually and romantically attracted to people of the same gender. You might also hear it used as an insult – 'that's gay!' – but this is something that LGBTQIA+ organizations are working very hard to address. 'Gay' is not a bad thing and should not be used as an insult.

Often, 'gay' is used as an umbrella term for the LGBTQIA+ community (gay bars, gay rights, Gay Pride, gay marriage etc.), and it is the most recognizable letter of the LGBT acronym. There are many people in the LGBTQIA+ community who speak out about this, as they believe it isn't inclusive of all people who should be under the umbrella. It's important to have these discussions, but also to remember that this is not an attack against gay men – rather, it's trying to expand the words we use to include everyone, including gay men.

Here are some people you may have heard of who identify as gay men:

Lil Nas X: a rapper, singer and songwriter who topped the charts with his country rap single *Old Town Road* for 19 weeks. He is the first artist to come out as gay while having a number one record.

Colton Haynes: an actor who has appeared in popular shows like *Arrow* and *Teen Wolf*. He came out as gay at 14, although he didn't come out publicly until 2016. He has also spoken out about the mental health challenges he has faced.

Billy Porter: an actor and singer who has a starring role in *Pose*, the hit TV show about New York City's African-American and Latino LGBTQ and gender-non-conforming ballroom culture scene in the 1980s. He once wore a black velvet tuxedo gown to the Oscars, stating, 'I'm not a drag queen. I'm a man in a dress'.

Bisexual

A bisexual person is a person (both cis and trans) who is attracted to more than one gender. Many bisexual people use the term 'bi' to describe themselves, so we will use the terms 'bisexual' and 'bi' interchangeably in this book.

When the word was first introduced just over a hundred years ago, it was used to describe someone who had sex with males and females ('bi' means 'two'). Since then, however, many people in the bisexual community have rejected this definition on the grounds that there are more than two sexes and genders (and that being bisexual is about romantic and sexual attraction rather than just sexual contact). According to bisexual activist Robyn Ochs, bisexuality is 'the potential to be attracted – romantically and/or sexually – to people of more than one sex and/or gender, not necessarily at the same time, not necessarily in the same way, and not necessarily to the same degree'.

Bisexual people are not necessarily attracted equally to all genders, and they do not have to have had sexual or romantic relationships with more than one gender in order to be bisexual. You may hear people refer to bisexual people who are in relationships as 'gay' or 'straight' (depending on who they are in a relationship with). This is incorrect. Just as a closeted gay man in a relationship with a woman is still gay, a bisexual person is still bisexual regardless of who they are currently in a relationship with.

Note: if someone is 'closeted', it means they are not yet open about their sexuality or gender. Someone could be completely closeted, where they are not open about their sexuality or gender even to themselves (e.g. a gay man may be in a relationship with a woman), or someone can be closeted around some people (e.g. open about their sexuality with friends, but not with certain family members). We'll look at 'coming out' (as in 'coming out of the closet' in a later chapter.

Here are some people you may have heard of who identify as bisexual:

Roxane Gay: a writer, professor and social commentator who writes about feminism, race, gender identity and sexuality. Her collection of essays, *Bad Feminist*, became a bestseller in 2014, and she has also published several novels.

Sara Ramirez: an actress, singer and songwriter who had a starring role in the hit show *Grey's Anatomy*. She came out as bisexual in 2016, and is an activist and campaigner for LGBTQIA+ rights. She also identifies herself as 'queer'.

Alan Cumming: an actor and singer who has starred in films like *Spy Kids* and *X-Men*, as well as starring in the West End and on Broadway. He has had prominent, long-term relationships with men and women, and became so tired of people asking him about his sexuality that he added a Frequently Asked Questions section to his official website.

Transgender

If a person is transgender, it means that their gender does not match the gender they were assigned at birth. Many transgender people describe themselves as 'trans' – the most common terms you are likely to hear are 'trans woman' (a woman who was assigned male at birth) and 'trans man' (a man who was assigned female at birth). As 'trans' is the term you are likely to hear in a lot of organizations and media, we will be using it throughout this book.

Gender identity is not the same thing as sexual orientation, although the communities and movements often overlap and work together. As a result, a trans person may also have another identity within the LGBTQIA+ umbrella. The difference between gender identity and sexuality is why the term 'transgender' was coined in the 1960s in place of the term 'transsexual' (which is no longer used to talk about the trans community).

Some trans people have dysphoria (a way to describe the pain, anxiety and confusion which can be felt if your gender identity does not match up with the sex you were assigned at birth) and will seek medical treatment, such as taking hormones and having surgery, as part of transitioning to their true gender. Other trans people may not have dysphoria and will not seek medical treatment as part of their transition. Whether or not a person has medical treatment does not change their gender identity.

A large number of autistic people identify as trans. There has been some research into why this may be, but with no conclusive results. Whatever the reason, it's important to recognize and respect the existence and experiences of trans autistic people.

Note: if your gender is the same as the sex you were assigned at birth (e.g. when I was born the doctors decided I was a girl, and I still identify as a girl today), then you are 'cisgender' or 'cis'. We'll be using the term 'cis' in this book.

Here are some people you may have heard of who identify as trans:

Laverne Cox: an actress, producer and activist who is best known for her role in the Netflix series *Orange Is the New Black*. She is the first openly transgender person to be nominated for a Primetime Emmy Award, and she has produced several successful documentaries about trans people and being trans. Her work as executive producer on *Laverne Cox Presents: The T Word* won her a Daytime Emmy Award in 2015.

Mj Rodriguez: an actress and singer who is known for her starring role in the hit drama *Pose*, which has the largest cast of transgender actors starring as series regulars in a scripted show. In 2019, she became the first trans woman of colour to play the role of Audrey in a major production of *Little Shop of Horrors*, stating, 'I'm simply an actress. I think any woman should be considered for this role. [My casting] shouldn't be something that's trending – it should be normal.'

Lewis Hancox: a comedian, writer, YouTuber and filmmaker who co-founded the trans filmmaking project My Genderation. His YouTube channel features comedy sketches in which he plays a variety of characters, with his most well-known being 'British Mum'. He also makes content around his experiences as a trans man, and his work with My Genderation focuses on trans people and their experiences. Find him at: www.youtube.com/lewishancox

Queer

'Queer' as an identity is different from the other identities in this chapter. This is because while some people identify only as queer, many different people (including gay people, bi people, trans people and asexual people) may identify as queer alongside their other identities.

'Queer' originally meant 'odd' or 'strange'. The ground-breaking gay TV show *Queer as Folk*, got its name from the phrase 'there's nowt so queer as folk' ('there's nothing as odd/strange as people'). Over a hundred years ago, it began to be used to describe people with non-heterosexual attraction and relationships, and in the 1980s it gained widespread use as an identity. It was also widely used in activism and by academics.

Queer is often used by people who don't identify as straight or gay, and is also often used by people who don't feel they fit into the rigid gender binary (the 'gender binary' is the idea that there are only two genders: male and female). Many people feel that it is the most inclusive umbrella term for anyone who is not straight and not cisgender. There are people who disagree, due to its widespread historic use as a derogatory term against LGBTQIA+ people. Others then argue that all of our commonly used identities were originally slurs that have been reclaimed by the community.

There is a continuing debate around the word 'queer'. Some people feel empowered by it. Some people feel insulted by it. But don't let this affect your own identity. If you identify with 'queer', then do not be afraid to use that term. If someone asks you not to refer to them as 'queer', then respect that.

Here are some people you may have heard of who identify as queer:

Elliot Page: an Oscar-nominated actor who has appeared in *Juno, Inception* and *Umbrella Academy*. They came out publicly as a lesbian in a speech at a Human Rights Campaign in 2014, and announced in December 2020 that they are trans and use he/him and they/them pronouns. He said: 'I love that I am trans. And I love that I am queer. And the more I hold myself close and fully embrace who I am, the more I dream, the more my heart grows and the more I thrive.'

Janelle Monáe: a singer, songwriter, rapper, actor and producer, famous for her concept albums *The ArchAndroid*, *The Electric Lady* and *Dirty Computer* and her roles in the films *Hidden Figures* and *Moonlight*. She is known for her signature style black and white tuxedos. She refers to herself as queer, but has stated she identifies with elements of bisexuality and pansexuality.

Jameela Jamil: an actor, radio presenter, television host and activist who is best known for her role as Tahani Al-Jamil in *The Good Place*. She has become well known for her activism, criticising body shaming and diet culture, and has spoken out about her experiences as a disabled woman. She came out 'officially' as queer in 2020, stating that it's 'scary as an actor to openly admit your sexuality, especially when you're already a brown female in your thirties'.

Intersex

If a person is intersex, it means they were born with biology that is not considered solely 'male' or 'female'. This may mean that they have variations in their chromosomes, their hormones, or their physical characteristics (often genitals). Not all intersex people like to be included within the LGBTQIA+ umbrella, and it is important to respect people's individual wishes. However, as there are many intersex people who do identify with the community, we are including this identity as part of this chapter.

You may have heard the term 'hermaphrodite' used to describe people who have both 'male' and 'female' characteristics. This is now considered an insult, and intersex people, organizations and scientists have successfully campaigned to drop the term from popular use. 'Intersex' is the accepted umbrella term to describe multiple different bodily variations: some of these are obvious at birth, some become more obvious during puberty and some may never be obvious (such as chromosomes). As such, many people may never know that they are intersex.

Some intersex people are assigned a sex at birth and are given surgery to make their physical characteristics match this (this has been called intersex genital mutilation by activists and organizations). While many of these people continue to identify with their assigned gender, some may not. This can cause severe distress for those who do not identify with their assigned gender. As a result, there are many questions about the continued use of surgery on intersex children, and many intersex organizations campaign against it. In 2015, Malta was the first country to ban these non-consensual surgeries.

Here are some people you may have heard of who identify as intersex:

Hanne Gaby Odiele: a supermodel who has worked for *Vogue*, and who revealed she is intersex in 2017. She has Androgen Insensitivity Syndrome, meaning that she has XY (typically 'male') chromosomes but her body doesn't respond properly to the hormone testosterone. She campaigns against intersex genital mutilation.

Hida Viloria: an author and human rights activist who wrote the acclaimed book, *Born Both: An Intersex Life*. She speaks, educates and campaigns extensively on intersex and non-binary issues and is a leading member of several intersex organizations. As a child, her parents chose to register and raise her as a girl without having any cosmetic genital surgeries, despite this being routinely recommended.

Asexual

An asexual person is a person (cis or trans) who experiences little to no sexual attraction. Many asexual people refer to themselves as 'ace', so we will use both 'asexual' and 'ace' in this book.

Some people who identify as asexual may also identify as 'aromantic' (not experiencing romantic attraction). Some people may therefore refer to themselves as 'a-spec' (on the asexual/aromantic spectrum). We'll look at the differences between sexual and romantic attraction in the next chapter.

It's important to understand the difference between asexuality and celibacy. If a person is celibate, it means that they have made a conscious decision to have no sexual contact. It does not mean that they don't experience sexual attraction. Asexuality means a lack of sexual attraction, rather than a lack of sexual contact. Many ace people do have, and enjoy, sex. Many ace people don't have sex. This doesn't make them any more or less asexual.

The Asexual Visibility and Education Network (AVEN) says:

> [t]here is no litmus test to determine if someone is asexual. Asexuality is like any other identity – at its core, it's just a word that people use to help figure themselves out. If at any

point someone finds the word asexual useful to describe themselves, we encourage them to use it for as long as it makes sense to do so.

Some people have argued that the term 'a-spec' was originally used by the autistic community (to refer to 'autistic spectrum'), and that asexual or aromantic people therefore shouldn't use it. However, many autistic people argue that they do not use, nor have they heard people use, the term 'a-spec', and it is generally agreed that asexual and aromantic people may use 'a-spec' to describe their identity.

Note: if you do feel sexual attraction or do not identify as asexual, then the commonly used to term to describe you is 'allosexual' or 'allo'. We'll be using the term 'allo' in this book.

Here are some people you may have heard of who identify as asexual:

Yasmin Benoit: a model, activist and writer who works in lingerie and alternative modelling and promotes the visibility of asexuality, aromanticism and LGBTQIA+ people of colour. In 2019, she hosted the first asexual themed bar at Pride in London and walked the runway in the London Queer Fashion Show. She is on the Board of Directors of AVEN.

Evan Edinger: an American-born YouTuber living in England, Evan is best known for his British vs American series, where he and other British YouTubers compare things like exams and healthcare systems between the two countries. He identifies as being on the asexual spectrum, including demisexual, and has made videos talking about this.

Emilie Autumn: a singer and musician who openly identifies as asexual. She describes her musical style as 'Fairy Pop', 'Fantasy Rock' or 'Victoriandustrial', and she performs on stage while playing the violin. She has said that while she is asexual, she has never 'disliked sex'.

Pansexual

A pansexual person is a person (either cis or trans) who is attracted to people regardless of gender. Some people who identify with this definition may still call themselves 'bisexual', but others feel that 'pansexual' is a term that fits better for them. It's important to use the terms that individual people are comfortable with.

The term 'pan' comes from the Ancient Greek word for 'all', and 'pansexual' and was originally used in 1917 by critics of Sigmund Freud, to mock the fact that early psychology seemed to be all about sex. It has since been reclaimed by members of the LGBTQIA+ community as a sexual identity. However, it's important to understand that 'pansexual' as a sexuality does not mean 'attracted to everyone' or 'has a lot of sex'. While some pansexual people may have a lot of sex with different people, others may have very little or no sex – neither is more or less pansexual than the other. 'Pansexual' simply means that gender is not a factor in attraction.

Pansexuality is sometimes called a more 'inclusive' version of bisexuality. This is because bisexuality is said to reinforce the strict gender binary (man and woman). However, many bisexual people disagree, as the definition of 'bisexual' as an identity has evolved as our understanding of gender has evolved. Although these conversations are ongoing, there is a general agreement on the difference between bisexuality and pansexuality:

- Bisexuality is attraction to more than one gender (which could mean all genders, or could mean some but not all genders).
- Pansexuality is attraction regardless of gender (which means gender isn't a fundamental factor in attraction).

Please do not let these discussions influence the terms that you use. Whether you feel more comfortable identifying as pansexual or bisexual, or using them both, you have the right to be proud of your identity.

Here are some people you may have heard of who identify as pansexual:

Joe Lycett: a comedian, television presenter and author who is best known for appearing on panel shows and hosting consumer right's show *Joe Lycett's Got Your Back*. He has spoken openly about his pansexuality in his comedy routines, as well as debunking myths and misconceptions about pansexuality.

Cara Delevingne: a model, actress and singer who has appeared in films like *Paper Towns* and *Suicide Squad*. She previously identified as bisexual, but spoke about being openly pansexual following a high-profile relationship with a woman. She says, 'However one defines themselves, whether it's "they" or "he" or "she", I fall in love with the person – and that's that.'

Jazz Jennings: coming out publicly as trans at the age of six, she has since become a star of her own reality series, *I Am Jazz*, and a popular YouTuber and LGBTQIA+ activist. She stated in an interview that she was still discovering who she is, as although she is mainly attracted to boys, she is also attracted to girls. In a 2014 YouTube video, she said that she is pansexual and loves people 'for their personality', regardless of their sexuality or gender.

Non-binary

A non-binary person is a person who does not identify exclusively as a man or a woman. You may also hear the term 'enby'. Many non-binary people see themselves as falling under the trans identity, as their gender identity does not match the gender they were assigned at birth. However, not all non-binary people agree with this, so it's important to respect personal preference.

The idea of a person being outside the gender binary has existed across many cultures for many years. Although 'non-binary' is a relatively recent term used to describe this, the belief in and acceptance of a 'third' gender has been seen throughout many non-Western civilizations. Some non-binary people may have gender confirmation surgeries, take hormones, or express themselves as more 'masculine' or 'feminine'. Others may not. But they are both still non-binary.

Non-binary can be used as an umbrella term for a variety of different gender identities, that may include:

- Bigender: identifying as two genders
- Trigender: identifying as three genders
- Pangender: identifying as many or all genders
- Agender: identifying as having no gender
- Genderfluid: moving between gender identities
- Third gendered: not identifying as a named gender.

As non-binary can be an umbrella term, it's important not to assume what pronouns a non-binary person may prefer. While some people prefer the gender-neutral 'they/them' pronouns, others may prefer gendered pronouns such as 'he/him' or 'she/her' (which may be because they identify as more masculine or feminine), or alternating gendered pronouns (if their gender is more fluid). There are also some alternative pronouns that people may feel more comfortable with, which can include: 'ze', 'sie', 'hir', 'co', and 'ey'.

Here are some people you may have heard of who identify as non-binary:

Owl and Fox Fisher: writers, filmmakers and non-binary trans activists, Owl and Fox Fisher are partners who have spoken extensively about being trans and non-binary. Fox is the co-founder of trans-led film project My Genderation with Lewis Hancox, and Owl and Fox maintain a joint YouTube channel. They also wrote the book *Trans Teen Survival Guide* for young trans people.

Sam Smith: a singer and songwriter, who won a Golden Globe and an Academy Award for their song *Writing's On The Wall* which was created for the James Bond film film Spectre. They came out as genderqueer in 2017, and in 2019 came out as non-binary and announced they were now using they/them pronouns: 'After a lifetime of being at war with my gender I've decided to embrace myself for who I am, inside and out.'

Asia Kate Dillon: an actor best known for their roles in *Orange Is the New Black* and *Billions*. In *Billions*, they played the first non-binary main character in North American Television, a role which earned them a Critic's Choice nomination. They have spoken about how they began removing gendered pronouns from their biography in 2015, and have stated that auditions for the role of Mason in *Billions* helped them to understand their gender.

And more...

As you can see, the LGBTQIA+ umbrella is very wide indeed. It includes many different people, of all sexualities and gender identities, and we have only been through some of them in this chapter.

There are so many other labels that wouldn't fit into this chapter. As more people explore their gender and sexuality, more labels are coined and celebrated to refer to people's experiences. Having a label that directly and accurately describes your experience of gender and sexuality can be extremely important.

You also don't have to only identify as one label. You can mix and match labels until you find a combination that fits your experience. We'll be looking more at the 'split attraction model' of sexuality in the next chapter, and how romantic attraction and sexual attraction can be different for different people.

If you're interested in finding out about more terms that we haven't had space to cover, there's an amazing book called *The A–Z of Gender and Sexuality* by Morgan Lev Edward Holleb.

If you do want to search further about the many different identities within the LGBTQIA+ community, please be aware that there are some people (particularly on the internet) who can be very dismissive and insulting about some of those identities. This includes claims that some people do not belong in the community. Ignore them. These people can be incredibly loud. But they are just a few people shouting very loudly.

It's important to remember most people don't share these views. Whatever identity fits you best, it is valid and it will be accepted.

As autistic people, it can be very helpful for us to have these definitions, explanations and histories when we are trying to understand our own identities. But it's probably not enough to figure it out completely. In the next chapter, we'll be looking at the processes involved in understanding our LGBTQIA+ identities, with some help from autistic people who have already been through it.

More information

Books

The A–Z of Gender and Sexuality: From Ace to Ze by Morgan Lev Edward Holleb

LGBTQ: The Survival Guide for Lesbian, Gay, Bisexual, Transgender, and Questioning Teens by Kelly Huegel Madrone

Links

Stonewall: www.stonewall.org.uk/help-advice/faqs-and-glossary/glossary-terms

Human Rights Campaign: www.hrc.org/resources/glossary-of-terms

Amnesty USA: www.amnestyusa.org/pdfs/toolkit_LGBTglossary.pdf

YouTube Videos

The ABC's of LGBT+ Series by Ash Hardell: http://bit.do/ABCsOfLGBT

In this series, which has been running for several years, Ash runs through different terms, definitions and identities that can be found in the LGBTQIA+ community. Some of these definitions change over the years, as knowledge of these things has evolved, so it's an excellent look at both what words mean and what it's like to learn new things about the words we use.

CHAPTER 2

Figuring It Out: Sexuality

Although sexuality and gender identity are both under the LGBTQIA+ umbrella, they are very different things. The process of figuring out your sexuality can be very different from the process of figuring out your gender identity. This is why the 'figuring it out' section is in two chapters.

In this chapter, we will look at the different journeys that autistic people may take to work out their sexuality.

Many of us have alexithymia – we can't identify and describe our emotions. This can make figuring out our sexuality, which is rooted in emotions and feelings towards other people, especially difficult.

This doesn't mean that we aren't able to know or make decisions about our sexuality or our gender identity. Many of us simply need support and safety in order to properly understand ourselves and our feelings.

It's important to remember that every person's story is different. There is no right way or wrong way to get to the point where you understand your sexuality. Many people will try out many different identities before they find the one that best fits them. Don't be afraid to change your mind if something doesn't feel right.

However, it's important to keep yourself safe.

The period where you are trying to figure out your sexual identity can be the most vulnerable time in your life. You may be tempted to put yourself in situations that you are not comfortable with as part of the 'figuring out' process. You may also be tempted to build unhealthy relationships during this time.

Please don't do this.

It should be possible for you to explore your sexuality without putting yourself at risk or in situations you don't want to be in. For more information on how to keep yourself as safe as possible, please have a look at the 'Out and About' and 'Relationships' chapters later on in this book.

Sexual attraction vs romantic attraction

It's generally agreed that there are two main types of attraction: sexual and romantic. Identifying what type of attraction you are feeling can be difficult. Sorting the different types of feelings you have, throughout your body, is a really important part of figuring out your sexuality.

Here is a quick definition of each:

- Sexual attraction: the feeling that you get when you want to have sexual contact with a specific other person.
- Romantic attraction: the feeling that you get when you

want to have a close, intimate relationship with a specific other person (that is not necessarily involving sex).

But, as with most things surrounding sexuality, it's not necessarily as simple as that. So we will go into slightly more detail on how to recognize these feelings.

Sexual attraction
Sexual attraction is that feeling you have in your body when you want to have sex with someone. It can be a mixture of physical and emotional. For example, if you are sexually attracted to someone, this may include feeling a tingle or throbbing somewhere in your body. It's most common to feel this in your genitals, but different people may have other sensitive spots where they feel this. You also might feel an excited flipping in your stomach, but this is also something you might feel when experiencing romantic attraction.

You may think: *I want to see this person naked, I want to touch this person, I want this person to touch me.* You may think more explicitly about what you would want to do with this person. You may fantasize about these things. If you masturbate, it can be helpful and interesting to take note of what you are imagining while feeling sexually aroused. Is it mostly men? Mostly women? Is it a mixture of different genders? Is it less about genders and more specifically about one person?

Sexual attraction doesn't necessarily have to be towards someone you know in real life. You may feel this way about a celebrity or a fictional character. As many autistic people struggle with social communication, often we will turn to fiction and fictional characters in order to understand the world and ourselves. There is nothing wrong with this. For example, you may figure out you are gay because you are sexually attracted to or fantasizing about a fictional character of the same gender as you in your favourite TV show.

It's important to remember that sexual attraction does *not* have to mean actually having sex. Your sexuality is not dependant on how many people (if any) of a certain gender you have had sex with. You may be sexually attracted to more than one gender, but only end up having sex with one person – you can still identify as having a sexuality attracted to multiple genders.

Sexuality is based on who you *want* to have sex with, rather than who you *do* end up having sex with.

Romantic attraction

Like with sexual attraction, romantic attraction is the feeling you get when you want to be close to someone. However, romantic attraction doesn't have to mean wanting to have sex with that person.

If you are romantically attracted to someone, it means that you have 'love'-type feelings towards them. Romantic attraction is often a desire to be around them as much as possible – you may want to spend time with them, to hold hands with them, to talk to them, to cuddle them, to snuggle on the couch watching TV with them. Thinking about that person may also make you feel very, very happy.

Although this is an emotional feeling, you can sometimes feel it in your body. When you think about this person, you may feel your stomach flipping (like it does on the morning of your birthday, or when you are sitting at the top of a rollercoaster waiting to go). You may feel your heart beating very fast when you're with them or thinking about them. You may also feel warm or tingly around them.

Everyone can feel romantic attraction in different ways.

You may feel similar feelings to some of your close friends. It can be difficult to work out whether what you're feeling is a friendship-type feeling or a romance-type feeling. Unfortunately, there aren't any solid ways to tell the difference. If you aren't sure what you're feeling, it can be helpful to try to organize your feelings: this may mean writing them down, finding someone you trust to talk to, and even having a chat with the person you have the feelings for (the last one might be difficult for you to do, so it might be worth trying the others first).

Whatever works best for you to sort out your feelings, make sure you are safe. Don't put yourself in any risky situations. Don't let yourself be isolated by someone you are feeling these things for. It can be very easy for your whole world to revolve around one person, and it's important to take a step back and make sure you have other people in your life.

How they work together
Often, sexual and romantic attraction are connected.

If you have a crush on someone, this may be a mixture of sexual and romantic attraction.

A lot of relationships have a mixture of romantic and sexual feelings. One may be stronger than the other, and the strength of each might change over time.

What starts as just sexual attraction can lead to romantic attraction. Some people can't feel sexual attraction until there are also romantic feelings there.

However, sexual attraction and romantic attraction don't necessarily have to go together.

You can have sexual feelings for someone without having romantic feelings. You can have a sexual relationship with someone without having any romantic feelings (this is perfectly okay, as long as you make sure you are safe).

You can also have romantic feelings for someone, as well as a successful romantic relationship, without having any sexual feelings (or any sexual contact).

Understanding your sexual and romantic attractions, and how they work together, is an important step in working out your sexuality. In the next section, we will look at how romantic and sexual attraction come together to shape your sexuality.

Sexual attraction, romantic attraction and sexuality
Sexual and romantic attraction work together differently in different people. Looking at your own feelings is the best way to find the identity that best suits you.

You may feel romantic attraction to more than one gender while only feeling sexual attraction to one. You may feel sexual attraction to many genders while only feeling romantic attraction to one. Some people can only feel sexual attraction if romantic attraction is also there.

Here are some examples of how sexual and romantic attraction work for different sexualities and identities on the LGBTQIA+ spectrum:

- If you are a woman (cis or trans) who only has romantic and sexual feelings for other women, then you may prefer to identify as a lesbian or gay.
- If you are a man (cis or trans) who only has romantic and sexual feelings for other men, then you may prefer to identify as gay.
- If you are romantically and sexually attracted to more than one gender, then you may prefer to identify as

bisexual or pansexual (see Chapter 1 for the different reasons people may prefer one over the other).

Some people believe in the idea of a 'split attraction'. This means that they see sexual and romantic attraction as two different identities. What matters is what works best for *you* in understanding your sexuality. I have found the split attraction model very helpful in understanding my identity.

- If you are sexually attracted to more than one gender, but are only romantically attracted to people of the same gender as you (and only want to have relationships with people of the same gender as you) then you may prefer to identify as gay or a lesbian. Some people who have these feelings may prefer to identify as a bi lesbian/gay or a pan lesbian/gay.
- If you do not feel sexually attracted to any gender, then you may prefer to identify as asexual. This does not have to mean that you don't feel romantic attraction. You may also feel sexual desire (the desire to have sex) but not feel specific sexual attraction to other people. This might mean you feel sexual desire, or get 'turned on' (or aroused) by watching sexual attraction occur between *other* people (e.g. in porn or on TV), but don't feel sexually attracted to specific people. Some people who identify as asexual do have sexual relationships, and other people who identify as asexual prefer not to have sexual relationships.
- You may not feel sexual attraction towards any gender, but feel romantically attracted to certain (or all) genders. Some people prefer to identify as asexual and heteroromantic (if romantically attracted to people of

the 'opposite' gender to themselves), asexual and homo-
romantic (if romantically attracted to people of the
same gender as themselves) or asexual and biromantic
(if romantically attracted to people of more than one
gender – some people may also prefer panromantic).

- If you only feel sexual attraction towards people that
you are also romantically attracted to, then you may
prefer to identify as demisexual. If you only feel sexually attracted to people in very specific circumstances,
then you may prefer to identify as somewhere on the
asexual spectrum (some people prefer to say they are
'a-spec') or as a 'grey ace'.

- Some people don't feel sexual attraction or romantic
attraction. If this sounds like you, then you may prefer
to identify as asexual and aromantic (some people prefer to identify as 'aroace'). It's important to remember
that if you don't feel sexual or romantic attraction, you
are not broken or in need of being fixed.

As autistic people, finding the right labels and language can
be very, very important for us. But it's not always something
that can be guaranteed with sexuality. And that's okay.

There are many people who know that their sexual and
romantic attraction definitely isn't 'straight', but they don't
quite feel comfortable deciding on a specific identity. Many
of these people will just call themselves 'queer'.

How do I figure it out?

You don't have to have sex in order to figure out who you are
attracted to. There are lots of different things that people do
to explore their sexuality that *don't* have to involve having sex.

Here are a few things you might do to help you figure out your sexuality.

Remember, everybody is different. Some people might do a lot of these things. Some people may not do any of these things. What's important is finding out what works for you, so that you can figure things out safely and comfortably.

Follow LGBTQIA+ people

Getting to know some famous or influential LGBTQIA+ people can be an incredibly important part of figuring out a) if you relate to them and b) why you relate to them.

In the age of social media, it's a lot easier to follow famous people and feel that we have a 'connection' to them, because they often share aspects of their lives with us. So, if a famous LGBTQIA+ person shares something (a picture, a video, a tweet, a story) that directly relates to their sexuality, and you think 'this is something I relate to', that could be a sign that you share that thing (your sexuality) in common with that person.

Of course, this isn't always true. I may relate to the experiences of a gay or lesbian celebrity, but that doesn't mean that I am gay – I am still bisexual. However, it is an indication that maybe I'm not straight, or that I am a part of the LGBTQIA+ community.

Many famous LGBTQIA+ people have interviews or books where they talk about their lives and experiences, which is a great way to learn about them and potentially connect with their experiences of sexuality.

Remember, though, just because you feel a connection with an LGBTQIA+ person, that doesn't necessarily mean that you must be LGBTQIA+ as well. Think about *what* it is that you are connecting to. If they are talking about being bullied for their sexuality, are you relating to that particular experience, or are you relating to their experience of being bullied? Sexuality is part of our everyday lives, after all, and we can share experiences linked to our sexuality without sharing a sexuality.

It might be helpful to break it down into a list of what they are saying, and which bits of what they are saying you specifically identify with.

'Famous' doesn't just have to mean actors or singers or politicians. There are many influential LGBTQIA+ people who have built up a following because of platforms like YouTube. YouTube can be a fantastic place to find LGBTQIA+ creators, making a whole range of videos about their lives and their experiences, and getting to 'know' them through their videos might be incredibly helpful.

We'll link to a few queer creators and their videos at the end of this chapter.

Media (books and films)
Mainstream media, such as television shows, films or books, can also be really helpful for figuring out your sexuality.

For example, seeing a gay character on a television show might be a part of working out that you are gay. Shows like *Andi Mack* on the Disney Channel feature a young teenager figuring out that he's gay, and coming out to his friends – if you are wondering if you might be gay, seeing this character's journey might help you to figure out your own sexuality.

It can be helpful to seek out shows, films and books that have LGBTQIA+ characters and storylines. Some media shows the story of LGBTQIA+ characters figuring out their own sexuality and coming out, whereas other media shows characters who are already out and may be in relationships.

However, remember that if you watch a programme and *don't* identify with a character, that doesn't mean that you aren't the same sexuality as that character. Every person is different, and therefore every character is different. There are many bisexual characters, for example, that I personally don't identify with, but that doesn't mean that I am not bisexual.

On streaming services like Netflix, you can search 'LGBT' in order to bring up films and shows in that category. You can also find lists of books that have LGBTQIA+ themes on websites like Goodreads.

Fandom and fanfiction

Many autistic people, including me, find themselves latching on to fictional worlds and fictional characters. Many of us, myself included again, will also get involved in fandom for specific films, books, TV shows, or characters, where we discuss these characters, talk about the storylines, and come up with 'headcanons' (our own versions of events or our own way of seeing the characters that aren't necessarily confirmed by the actual canon – the officially accepted story – of the show).

Fandom is the space where I figured out my sexuality. As a teenager, I latched on to a character called Ianto Jones in the TV show *Torchwood*; this character was bisexual and through that character I began to explore my own feelings around sexuality. I also found that, as the show itself was very queer, I was surrounded by a lot of other fans who weren't straight, and this community helped me to figure things out.

You may find yourself 'headcanoning' certain characters as different sexualities (e.g. there is a prominent popular headcanon about Steve Rogers, Captain America, being bisexual). Talking about the reasons why you have this headcanon, and the clues and signs in the material, can also help you to explore the reasons why you think *you* may be a particular sexuality.

Reading and writing fanfiction can also be an incredibly powerful thing. When you read fanfiction about specific characters, particularly focused on a character's sexuality or relationships, you can relate to the experiences, and the characters, and that may be helpful in terms of figuring out your sexuality. Writing fanfiction, whether you share it publicly or not, can also be a tool to work through how you are feeling. It can sometimes be easier to explore different feelings and experiences by writing about them through a character that you relate to.

'Shipping' is when you are a fan of a particular sexual/romantic relationship in a story. If you 'ship' characters, you want them to be together (the word 'ship' comes from the word 'relationship'). This may mean an established relationship, where the characters are together in the story, or it may mean shipping characters who are not in a relationship. Shipping may be the first place that you are able to explore the idea of a same-gender relationship, and talking/writing about it can be a safe way of sorting out the things in your own head. Shipping can also be used in a similar way to porn or erotica, (which we'll look at in the next section) with a lot of fanfiction being sexual in nature, to help you figure out what your sexual attractions are and how you feel about the idea of sex as an LGBTQIA+ person.

It's also quite common for women who identify as queer to ship two male characters together as a part of exploring their sexuality. Some people report that shipping two female characters was a bit too 'real' or close to be a comfortable way of exploring their sexuality, whereas shipping male characters was close enough to be useful but not too close to be uncomfortable. It's also the case that male characters are often more developed than female characters (unfortunately), so many women will develop connections to ships involving two men and then realize that this was because they are also not straight. Some people may realize that it's more about identifying with the emotional connections than feeling sexual attraction to the characters, and from that may realize that they identify as ace or demisexual.

Whatever the reason, it's important to remember that if you are a woman questioning her sexuality, it is not abnormal for you to be shipping two male characters as a part of figuring this out. In the same way, if you are a man questioning his sexuality, it is not abnormal for you to be shipping two female characters as a part of figuring this out. There is no right or wrong way to use fandom, shipping and fanfiction to help figure out this part of yourself.

A lot of fandom takes place online, so be careful about protecting your privacy and keeping yourself safe. We'll have more information on staying safe online in our chapter on being out and about in LGBTQIA+ spaces.

Porn

Pornography is when there are photographs and videos/films of people having sex and performing sex acts. It is available quite easily on the internet, so you might have already seen some. A lot of young people have. There is nothing shameful about watching porn. There are lots of different types of porn, including same-sex porn, and it can help to give you some idea of what you are attracted to (what 'turns you on').

It's useful to examine what you are thinking about while watching porn: are you feeling attracted to the performers, are you imagining yourself in the situation (as if it was happening to you), or are you just feeling aroused by the situation or scene that's being shown? For example, if you are turned on by the thought of the thing on screen happening to you, who are you imagining doing it? Are you imagining yourself in the place of a certain performer in the scene? Are you feeling turned on by the thought of that specific performer doing something to you? Do you prefer porn with more backstory than just sex, so you feel like you 'know' the characters more? Or is it more the case of 'this would be nice, but I'm not really imagining either the performers or anyone in particular doing it to me'?

There's a difference between desire (being turned on by the idea of sex) and attraction (being turned on by the idea of sex with a specific person). If you think you might be asexual, but find yourself being turned on by porn, this doesn't mean that you aren't asexual – you may feel sexual desire when thinking about the actions, but not sexual attraction for the people doing the actions.

Your sexuality is not defined by the type of porn you prefer, but thinking about porn in this way can help you ask questions about what you're feeling about sex, desire and attraction.

However, it's very important to remember that porn is not real. It's useful to watch porn in the same way you watch a film or a TV show: it is scripted by writers and performed by actors. Real sex will not be like the sex you see in porn. People's bodies do not usually look like they do in porn.

It's also important to remember that most lesbian porn, which shows two women having sex with each other, is not written or performed by women who are attracted to women. A lot of porn treats women like objects and can be very violent to them. A lot of the sex that you see in porn, particularly more extreme porn, would be abusive if it were to happen in real life. As a result of this, some gay women may prefer to watch porn involving sex acts between two men – not because they are sexually attracted to men, but because it's less likely to show women being treated badly.

A lot of mainstream porn is also very transphobic, using slurs to describe trans people (particularly trans women) and treating trans bodies like a fetish (something 'out of the ordinary' that turns people on). Whether you are figuring out your gender or not, please remember that these depictions are harmful and not representative of trans people.

There are some companies that are now making more 'ethical' porn. There are porn companies that are run by women who are attracted to women *for* women who are attracted to women. There are porn companies that want to make more 'feminist' porn which treat women with respect. There are porn companies that are making porn that features trans people without being transphobic or harmful. And there are porn companies that are working to show more realistic sex.

This type of porn is unlikely to be available on the free porn sites, so you may not be able to access it. Remember to protect yourself if you try to access this type of porn: any subscriptions or payments may be visible to your parents or guardians, and not everyone's parents or guardians are happy about them watching porn (particularly non-straight porn). Put your safety first.

If you are watching porn as a way of working out what turns you on or what makes you orgasm, you are not strange and you are not a bad person. Just remember that porn is not real sex, and you should treat it as fiction.

If you find yourself watching *a lot* of porn, or you start craving porn on a regular basis, then it's a good idea to speak to someone you trust. Porn addiction is a real problem. As autistic people, we can be more vulnerable to becoming addicted to things. If you aren't sure if you're watching too much, start making a note every time you watch porn or find yourself wanting to watch it. If you have to make a note every day, stop watching porn (if you can) or speak to someone who might be able to help.

Erotica

Erotica, or erotic fiction, is like the written version of porn. However, unlike a lot of mainstream porn, erotica can go into more detail on the feelings, thoughts and people behind the sex acts. This might let you connect with certain characters and their experiences in ways that mainstream porn doesn't.

Erotica can also be available in audiobook form, which can make it more accessible. If you struggle with reading books, audiobooks are a great way to access this type of erotic story. It might also provide a different experience – hearing someone read erotica to you, rather than reading it to yourself, can give you a different feeling.

There are many erotic books published by 'own voices' authors – authors who have the lived experience of the topics that are being covered. This may mean an erotic book about a bisexual autistic woman that is actually written by a bisexual autistic woman. There is a large community of own voices authors on social media, often using the hashtag #OwnVoices.

Many own voices authors self-publish, and their work can be found on sites like Amazon. Their stories can be physically bought or downloaded onto devices like phones. Some (but not all) may also be available as audiobooks, if you find this easier to process than reading.

You can also access erotica for free on the internet, with some sites acting as platforms for people to upload their erotic stories. However, as with mainstream porn, remember that these sites are often not vetted, so content may contain harmful messages and will often not be produced by people of that sexuality or experience. If you encounter erotica that includes children (anyone who is under the age of 18 counts as a child), is especially violent, or even just makes you feel uncomfortable, it's important to stop reading.

Sex and relationships
At the end of all this, you might find that the best way for you to explore your sexuality is by having sex or getting into relationships (sexual or otherwise). If so, remember that there's no rush to put a label on your identity. Don't do anything you don't feel ready for and aren't completely happy doing. We'll have more information on how to have healthy and safe sexual/romantic relationships in Chapters 6 and 7.

How do I know for sure?

The annoying thing about sexuality is that there isn't always a way to know for sure.

Some people may know instinctively which identity fits them best. I know people who have known since childhood who they are attracted to, and who have comfortably identified with one specific label from the moment they learned about it. If this is your experience, you don't have to question why this is, or whether you need to 'experiment' to find out more – if you know what makes you comfortable and happy, you stick with that.

For some other people, it's a bit less clear cut. I know people who now identify as a completely different sexuality from when they were younger. This doesn't have to mean that how they felt as a teenager or young adult was wrong. It just means that their understanding of who they are has changed over time.

You may not be sure until you actually have sex. You may have some sexual or romantic experiences with people of a certain gender and decide that, actually, it isn't for you. However, remember to be safe – you don't *have* to have sex or rush into a relationship in order to 'test' your sexuality, so only do what feels right and comfortable for you.

For some people, a change in how they identify may come because they realize they haven't been honest with themselves – many people, who grew up without being taught about non-straight sexualities, or who were made to believe that anything other than being straight was shameful, may not have fully realized or accepted their sexuality until they were much older. For example, my mum didn't realize she was gay until she was 50 years old.

Although this still happens today for some people, we know that the world is much more open and accepting of LGBTQIA+ identities. That is why this book is able to exist. But this just shows that there are many people who are still working themselves out, well into adulthood. There's nothing wrong with not knowing or changing your mind.

Sometimes, people change how they identify because they learn new words and labels that better fit their experiences. For example, someone who knew they weren't straight or gay, but didn't know that things like 'bisexual' and 'pansexual' exist, may have just assumed they were straight. That doesn't mean they were straight – it just means they didn't have the knowledge or the words to describe their feelings. It's okay to change how you identify if you come across new, better words that you find fit you better.

However, it's important not to use your own experiences to attack other people's identities. For example, if you used to identify as bisexual, and then realized you are actually gay, this doesn't mean that everyone who identifies as bisexual is actually gay. It can be tempting to project our own experiences onto other people, but we need to work hard not to do this.

Remember that everybody has a different experience and it's important to respect other people's identities.

I know people who, well into adulthood, still don't have a single word they feel comfortable using to describe their sexuality. If you are struggling to find a word that fits you best, then you may be comfortable saying 'I don't know, and that's okay'. You are allowed to do this. Many people find that labels are helpful. But if you are finding the labels difficult or restrictive, then you don't have to choose one.

Where gender identity comes in

Although I have separated sexuality and gender into two categories, gender identity is really important when it comes to sexuality.

For some people, figuring out their sexuality goes hand in hand with figuring out their gender. For example, before realizing their gender, a straight trans woman may have presented as a gay cis man. Likewise, before transitioning, a gay trans man may have presented as a straight cis woman. A straight person whose partner comes out as trans (including non-binary or gender fluid) may remain with their partner and begin to identify as bisexual or pansexual. A lesbian whose partner transitions may decide to identify as a bi or pan lesbian. I also know people who continue to identify as gay after they realize that they are non-binary or gender fluid.

Understanding of your sexuality may evolve along with the understanding of your gender identity. It may also evolve along with the understanding of the gender identities of the people around you (particularly the people you find attractive).

However your own journey to understanding your sexuality goes, figuring out your gender may be an important part of it.

And that's what we'll be looking at in the next chapter.

More information

Books

Gender Identity, Sexuality and Autism by Eva A. Mendes and Meredith R. Maroney

Queer: A Graphic History by Meg-John Barker and Jules Scheele

LGBTQ: The Survival Guide for Lesbian, Gay, Bisexual, Transgender, and Questioning Teens by Kelly Huegel Madrone

The Pride Guide: A Guide to Sexual and Social Health for LGBTQ Youth by Jo Langford

Links

ReachOut: https://au.reachout.com/articles/understanding-your-sexuality

Childline: www.childline.org.uk/info-advice/your-feelings/
sexual-identity/sexual-orientation

The Asexual Visibility and Education Network (AVEN): www.
asexuality.org/?q=general.html

YouTube videos

Having Pride by Thomas Sanders: http://bit.do/Having-Pride

End of Pride Month Q & Gay by Thomas Sanders and Friends:
http://bit.do/Q-And-Gay
Thomas himself identifies as gay, but in this series, and his other
videos, he features a lot of his friends who talk about their different
experiences with gender and sexuality.

The Sex Education You Never Had *PRIDE EDITION* by Ellbat: http://
bit.do/Sex-Education-You-Never-Had
In this hour-long video, Ellbat (with an appearance by Fox Fisher)
answers lots of questions about all things LGBTQIA+, including
common questions around figuring out sexuality (e.g. 'This is
something that's happened to me, does it mean I'm bisexual?'). It
includes sections on being gay, lesbian, bisexual and asexual, and
a general section on sexuality. You can find the questions you
need answering, and what time they appear in the video, in the
description box for easy access to information.

The Neverending Queer-y: My Queer Ace Journey by Vesper (Queer as
Cat): http://bit.do/The-Neverending-Queery
In this video, Vesper goes back through old YouTube videos and
uses them to document the last decade of their journey with gender and sexuality. It includes a look at changing labels, evolving
identities and the ongoing process of figuring stuff out.

Basically I'm Gay by Daniel Howell: http://bit.do/Basically-Im-Gay
In this video, Dan talks about the journey to figuring out his sexuality, his relationship with different labels and how he got to where he is now.

Realising We're Gay by Jessica Kellgren-Fozard: http://bit.do/Realising-Were-Gay
In this video, Jessica and her wife Claudia talk about how they realized they were gay.

CHAPTER 3

Figuring It Out: Gender

A s a cisgender woman (my gender identity matches the sex I was assigned at birth – the doctors looked at my body and said 'she's a girl', and my gender identity matches this), I have worked very hard to make sure that this chapter is built on the experiences, writing, work and voices of trans people.

What does it mean to be transgender?

If you are transgender, or trans (we will use 'trans' in its shortened form in this book), it means that the gender you identify as does not match up with the sex you were assigned at birth.

This may mean that you were assigned male at birth, but you realize you are actually a woman. People who have this experience are 'trans women' (it is important to remember that they are as much real women as women who were assigned female at birth).

This may mean that you were assigned female at birth, but you realize you are actually a man. People who have this experience are 'trans men' (it is important to remember that they are as much real men as men who were assigned male at birth).

It may also mean that you were assigned female or male at birth, but realize that you don't fit into either category. People who have this experience may identify with a number of different identities: non-binary (being neither a man nor a woman), gender fluid (moving between genders) and agender (not having a gender) being some of the most common. We will look at these, and other identities, a little bit later on in this chapter.

As with sexuality, different people have different experiences of figuring out their gender. Some people know from their earliest memories that they are not the sex they were assigned at birth. Other people don't realize until much later in life. Some people experiment with several different genders and labels before they find one that they feel suits them. Others prefer not to define their gender at all, as there isn't a label that seems to fit them properly.

All of these experiences are valid. Your experience may not be the same as someone else's. That doesn't mean that you are 'doing it wrong'. It also doesn't mean that anyone else is 'doing it wrong'.

What does gender feel like?

This is a very difficult thing to describe. Everyone has a slightly different experience with their gender.

If you google this question, a lot of the answers, explanations and advice will be very complicated. You may also find a lot of disagreements based on what angle the person is coming from. This is very normal, because gender is a very personal experience.

Many autistic people have complicated relationships with their gender. This is okay.

It's okay if you look something up and don't understand what people are talking about. There is a lot of academic study around gender, and a lot of this is very complicated. Don't let this impact or lessen your experiences. This is mainly about how *you* feel – you don't have to read a long, wordy, complicated academic text in order to decide what gender feels like for you.

A good (but not perfect) way to start thinking about the way we experience gender is to look at the 'gender unicorn'. This splits gender into three: gender identity, gender expression and assigned sex at birth.

- Assigned sex – the sex that you were assigned at birth (usually by the doctors looking at what genitals you have).
- Gender identity – what you feel (whether you feel like a man, a woman, or both, or neither).
- Gender expression – how you like to express what you feel (through clothes, hair, make up etc.).

I encourage you to grab some coloured pencils and start filling in the diagram opposite for yourself. Pick a colour for the different arrows, and then start filling in the picture of the unicorn with those colours to represent how you feel. Have a think about the different things, what they mean, and

The Gender Unicorn

● Gender Identity
Female/Woman/Girl
Male/Man/Boy
Other Gender(s)

◯ Gender Expression
Feminine
Masculine
Other

Sex Assigned at Birth
Female   Male   Other/Intersex
◯   ◯   ◯

♡ Sexually Attracted To
Women
Men
Other Gender(s)

♡ Emotionally Attracted To
Women
Men
Other Gender(s)

Graphic by:
TSER
Trans Student Educational Resources

To learn more go to:
www.transstudent.org/gender

Design by Landyn Pan
Illustration by Anna Moore

how you feel about them. Mix colours together if you need to. Have a rubber ready in case you change your mind about anything or want to change it. Remember, this is just a way for you try things out and play around with ideas. If it doesn't work for you, or stresses you out, you don't have to do it.

We'll have a look at all of these aspects of gender separately now.

Assigned sex

When we are born, we are 'assigned' a sex. This is usually based on what genitals we have. A baby that has a penis will likely be classed as a 'boy' or 'male', and a baby that has a vagina will likely be classed as a 'girl' or 'female'.

You might hear people call this 'biological sex'.

It's important to remember that many scientists agree that the idea of 'biological sex' is much more complicated. We traditionally think of 'biological sex' as being binary (boy or a girl) and very clear cut (vagina = girl, penis = boy), but there are many other things that could also indicate 'biological sex' (hormones, chromosomes etc.). These are never measured in most people.

Biology can be very complicated, and this isn't shown in the way we assign sex to babies at birth.

Many trans people will not refer to themselves as 'biologically female' or 'biologically male'. Even if a woman was assigned male at birth, they *are* a woman and therefore their body is biologically a woman's body. Even if a man was assigned female at birth, they *are* a man and therefore their body is biologically a man's body.

This is why we won't be using the term 'biological sex' in this book. But it's important you know it, as many people do still use it when talking about gender.

Gender identity

Gender identity is your own personal sense of your own gender. It's how *you* feel about your own gender, and what gender you feel you are.

This may match up with the sex you were assigned by doctors at birth, or it might be different. For example, I was assigned female at birth, and I have never questioned that I am a woman. I have always just known that this is the gender I am, and that it just happens to match what the doctors decided about me when I was born.

In the same way, you may have been assigned as male or female at birth but know that you are a different gender.

Many trans people say that they just 'know' that they are a different gender to the gender they were assigned at birth. As a young child, you may have told your parents or caregivers that you were a different gender to the gender you were being told you were. This doesn't mean that you necessarily *are* trans, but it's something to look into and think about if you are questioning your gender.

For some people, understanding their gender identity can come a little bit later or take a little bit more digging. Some trans people report that they always felt that *something* was different, but they weren't able to work out what it was. Other trans people say that they never really identified with a particular gender, or identified with a gender other than the two binary gender options they were given (male and female).

Everyone's gender identity is individual to them. It's okay to take time and try things out while working out what your personal gender identity is.

Gender expression

Your gender expression is how you decide to show, or feel

most comfortable showing, the world your gender identity. Different societies have different traditions around what is 'masculine' (associated with being a man) and what is 'feminine' (associated with being a woman).

For example, if you are a woman, you may express your gender by wearing clothes and colours that are seen as 'feminine' in our society (dresses, flowery patterns, pink colours etc.).

Or, you may be a woman who prefers to express her gender in a different way (having short hair, wearing colours like blue etc.).

If you express your gender in a way that is different from what your society expects, you might be described as 'gender non-conforming'. Many autistic people identify as gender non-conforming because it can be harder for us to understand or follow expectations of what we're 'supposed' to do.

Gender expression can be connected to your gender identity. For example: if you are assigned male at birth, but find yourself more drawn to expressing your gender in a more 'feminine' way (for example: wearing dresses, having long hair, playing with dolls), you may realize that you are actually a girl.

However, gender expression is not always linked to gender identity. A child who plays with dolls or prefers dresses is not necessarily a girl, just as a child who plays with toy cars and prefers trousers is not necessarily a boy. Your gender identity may match the sex you were assigned at birth (you may have been assigned as a girl at birth, and know that you are a girl), but your gender expression may not be traditionally 'girly'. You can be cisgender *and* gender non-conforming.

Also, you can be transgender *and* gender non-conforming. You can be a trans woman (a woman who was assigned male at birth), and yet still be 'butch' or traditionally masculine. You can be a trans man (a man who was assigned female at birth), and yet still be traditionally feminine. While gender identity and gender expression can work closely with each other, they are not always as linked as you might think.

So, if you were assigned male at birth, but *know* that you are a girl, it doesn't make you any less of a girl if you don't like playing with dolls or wearing dresses. Gender identity is how you *feel* and what you *are*. Gender expression is how you prefer to express that identity.

As autistic people, our sensory experiences can play a huge part in how we express our gender. Do you prefer trousers and short hair to skirts and long hair because you are a boy, or because you really don't like how skirts and long hair feel? An autistic trans woman may prefer trousers and short hair for the same reasons, but this doesn't mean that she is not a trans woman. Lots of autistic people have sensory issues around clothes, which may impact how they express their gender.

It's okay to take the time to work out *why* you express your gender identity a certain way, and whether or not this means your gender identity is at odds with your assigned sex at birth.

What is gender dysphoria?

Many trans people experience gender dysphoria. This is a way to describe the pain, anxiety and confusion which can be felt if your gender identity does not match up with the sex you were assigned at birth. You can be diagnosed as having gender dysphoria by a mental health professional.

Gender dysphoria can be physical – this means it relates to your body, and the idea of your body being 'wrong' for your gender identity. For example, if you are a trans woman, having a penis may make you feel dysphoric because women aren't expected to have penises. There may be a sense that you are not supposed to have this part of your body, or you may wish that you had another body part in its place. In this way, having body features that don't match your gender identity may cause you pain and anxiety.

Gender dysphoria can be social – this means it relates to ways in which society separates the genders into 'man' and 'woman', such as clothes, hobbies or what pronouns are used. For example, if you are a non-binary person, being referred to with gendered pronouns ('he' or 'she') may make you feel dysphoric because they assign you a gender that you don't identify with. Being misgendered like this may cause pain and anxiety. Another example may be that, if you are a trans man, wearing a dress may make you dysphoric because dresses are socially recognized as something women wear. In this way, wearing clothes that suggest that you are a different gender to how you identify can cause pain and anxiety.

Not everyone experiences gender dysphoria the same way. A trans man, for example, may experience gender dysphoria around having breasts, but not around having a vagina. Other trans men may experience gender dysphoria around both. For other trans men, simply being able to dress in a way that society sees as 'masculine' and using he/him pronouns may be enough to quell gender dysphoria.

Some people may have medical treatment, such as taking hormones or having surgery to alter their body, in order to overcome gender dysphoria. Other people may change their pronouns and how they present their gender (clothing, hair, make up etc.) in order to overcome gender dysphoria. Every person's experience of gender dysphoria is unique. You are allowed to take time to question whether you have gender dysphoria and, if so, what your gender dysphoria focuses on.

Some trans people may not experience gender dysphoria at all. They may not feel distress or pain about their gender identity. This does not mean you are less trans than someone who does. Being 'really' trans is not about how much you have suffered compared to others.

Some people may end up experiencing gender euphoria – this is the comfort, joy and even pleasure that can be found in your gender. This may be related to being gendered correctly by people (people you know or strangers), being able to present as the gender you identify as, or getting to the point where you feel physically like the gender that you are.

Remember: there are so many different ways of feeling gender dysphoria, and so many different people have so many different experiences with it. As a cis woman, I have experienced none of these, and therefore this section will always be inadequate. It's important that you reach out to trans people to find out more, using books and blogs written by trans people about their experiences, YouTube videos by trans people talking about dysphoria, and forums where you can speak to other trans people (if they're happy to do so) about their dysphoria. You will get a much better idea and understanding of dysphoria from them than from my explanation here. This is only a very basic introduction, and trans people are the only voices that can have this conversation properly.

How do I figure it out?

There are no set rules when it comes to figuring out your gender. Everyone has a slightly different experience. But there are things you can do to help figure it out.

Remember that everybody is different. Some people might

do a lot of these things. Some people may not do any of these things. What's important is finding out what works for you, so that you can figure things out safely and comfortably.

Ask yourself questions

Asking yourself questions, and taking time to think about the answers, can be really helpful if you're figuring out your gender identity. You might prefer to just think about the answers, or you might want to try and write down what you're thinking about the answers. Sometimes making notes can really help you figure things out.

Here are some questions you might want to think about:

- Have you ever felt as if you don't have the same experience of gender as other people you know?
- Have you ever thought about what it would be like if other people saw you as a different gender (including using certain pronouns)?
- If you think of yourself as an older person, how do you see yourself? Do you see yourself as an old man, an old woman, or something different?
- Do you have persistent thoughts about wanting to physically change your body to look like a different sex?
- Do you connect with the stories/experiences of trans people in the public eye?

Answering yes to any, or all, of these questions doesn't necessarily mean you are trans. This is why you might want to make lots of notes, or write your feelings down as you have them, to try and figure out how you feel.

However, if you do find yourself agreeing with these

statements, you might want to think about whether you might be trans.

Follow LGBTQIA+ people

Getting to know some famous or influential trans and non-binary people can be an incredibly important part of figuring out a) if you relate to them and b) why you relate to them.

In the age of social media, it's a lot easier to follow famous people and feel that we have a 'connection' to them, because they often share aspects of their lives with us. So, if a famous trans or non-binary person shares something (a picture, a video, a tweet, a story) that directly relates to their gender, and you think 'this is something I relate to', that could be a sign that you have that thing (your gender identity) in common with that person.

Of course, this isn't always true. I may relate to some of the experiences of a famous trans or non-binary person, but that doesn't mean that I'm trans – I am still definitely cisgender. However, it's important to remember that I have never questioned my identity as a cisgender woman, and so my experiences in this area are not as relevant as yours.

Many famous trans and non-binary people have interviews or books where they talk about their lives and experiences, which is a great way to learn about them and potentially connect with their experiences of gender. You can often also get these in audiobook form.

Remember, though, just because you feel a connection with a trans or non-binary person, that doesn't necessarily mean that you must be trans or non-binary as well. Think about *what* it is that you are connecting to. If they are talking about being bullied for their gender, are you relating to that particular experience, or are you relating to their experience of being bullied? Gender is a part of our everyday lives, after all, and we can share experiences linked to our gender and gender identity without sharing the exact same experience of gender.

It might be helpful to break it down into a list of what they are saying, and which bits of what they are saying you specifically identify with.

'Famous' doesn't just have to mean actresses or singers or politicians. There are many influential LGBTQIA+ people who have built up a following because of platforms like YouTube. YouTube can be a fantastic place to find LGBTQIA+ creators, making a whole range of videos about their lives and their experiences, and getting to 'know' them through their videos might be incredibly helpful.

We'll link to a few trans creators and their videos at the end of this chapter.

Media (books and films)

Mainstream media, such as television shows, films or books, can be a really helpful part of figuring out your gender identity.

For example, seeing a trans character on a television show might be a part of working out that you are trans. Shows like *Orange Is the New Black* on Netflix, which features a trans woman played by a trans actress, and depicts aspects of her journey as she transitioned, might help you to figure out your own gender identity if you are wondering if you might be trans.

It can be helpful to seek out shows, films and books that have characters and storylines around gender identity. Some pieces of media show the story of trans characters figuring out their own gender and coming out, whereas others show characters who are already out and living their lives.

However, remember that if you watch a programme and *don't* identify with a character, that doesn't mean that you aren't trans in the way that the character is. Every person is different, and therefore every character is different. Just as there are many cis women that I, a cis woman, do not identify with, so you may not necessarily identify closely with a trans character whose experiences mirror your own.

You might also find yourself identifying closely with cis-gender characters (e.g. if you think you may be a trans man, you may find yourself identifying with cis male characters), which might be helpful in terms of figuring out your gender.

On streaming services like Netflix, you can search 'LGBT' in order to bring up films and shows in that category. You can also find lists of books that have LGBTQIA+ themes online.

Fandom and fanfiction

Many autistic people, including me, find ourselves latching on to fictional worlds and fictional characters. Many of us, myself included again, will also get involved in fandom for specific films, books, TV shows, or characters, where we discuss these characters, talk about the storylines, and come up with 'headcanons' (our own versions of events, or our own way of seeing the characters).

As well as connecting closely with trans characters, as previously discussed, there are other ways that fandom might be a helpful place to figure out your gender identity.

You may find yourself 'headcanoning' certain characters as either different genders or as trans (e.g. there was a promi-nent popular headcanon about Peter Parker, Spiderman, being a trans boy). Talking about the reasons why you have this headcanon, and the clues and signs in the material, can also help you to explore the reasons why you think *you* may be a particular gender identity.

Reading and writing fanfiction can also be an incredibly powerful thing. When you read fanfiction about specific characters, particularly focused on a character's gender, you can relate to the experiences, and the characters, and that may be helpful in terms of figuring out your gender identity. Writing fanfiction, whether you share it publicly or not, can also be a tool to work through how you are feeling. It can sometimes be easier to explore different feelings and experiences by writing about them through a character that you relate to.

If you are transitioning, or thinking of transitioning, your sexuality might change or be viewed differently, so talking/ writing about different types of relationships from different perspectives may be an important part of understanding how your gender relates to your sexuality. For example, a trans man may ship two male characters together as a part of exploring the idea of being a man and what their sexuality is as a man.

You may also connect with other autistic trans people though fandom, who may be able to help you understand your experiences. However, a lot of fandom takes place online, so be careful about protecting your privacy and keeping your-self safe. We'll have more information on staying safe online in the chapter on being out and about in LGBTQIA+ spaces.

Transitioning
At the end of all this, you might find that the best way for you to explore your gender is by having a go at transitioning and living as the gender you are exploring. If so, remember that

there's no rush to do anything. Don't do anything you don't feel ready for and aren't completely happy doing. We'll have a whole chapter on transitioning later in the book.

How do I know for sure?

Like with sexuality, it's very difficult to answer this question. I *know* that I am a woman. You might *know* that you are a man, even if the doctors told your parents you were a girl when you were born. Someone else might *know* that they are neither a man nor a woman. But that doesn't mean we can necessarily explain exactly how we know that for sure.

Many people who go through the process of figuring out their gender and decide that they are trans will then start to transition. Transitioning is the process where you start to live your life as your true gender identity. It's okay to continue exploring your gender even as you transition, or even after you have transitioned.

We'll be looking more at transitioning in an upcoming chapter. In the meantime, we'll consider how to safely tell the people around you (friends, family, co-workers, medical professionals, carers etc.) about your sexuality or your gender identity.

Books

Gender Identity, Sexuality and Autism by Eva A. Mendes and Meredith R. Maroney

Trans Teen Survival Guide by Owl and Fox Fisher

Uncomfortable Labels: My Life as a Gay Autistic Trans Woman by Laura Kate Dale

Trans: A Memoir by Juliet Jacques

LGBTQ: The Survival Guide for Lesbian, Gay, Bisexual, Transgender, and Questioning Teens by Kelly Huegel Madrone

The Pride Guide: A Guide to Sexual and Social Health for LGBTQ Youth by Jo Langford

Links

Mermaids: https://mermaidsuk.org.uk/young-people

Childline: www.childline.org.uk/info-advice/your-feelings/sexual-identity/transgender-identity

ReachOut: https://au.reachout.com/articles/everything-you-need-to-know-about-gender

YouTube videos

Having Pride by Thomas Sanders: http://bit.do/Having-Pride

End of Pride Month Q & Gay by Thomas Sanders and Friends: http://bit.do/Q-And-Gay
Thomas himself identifies as gay, but in this series, and his other videos, he features a lot of his friends who talk about their different experiences with gender and sexuality.

The Sex Education You Never Had *PRIDE EDITION* by Ellbat: http://bit.do/Sex-Education-You-Never-Had
In this hour-long video, Ellbat (with an appearance by Fox Fisher) answers lots of questions about all things LGBTQIA+, including common questions around figuring out your gender. It includes sections on being trans and being non-binary. You can find the questions you need answering, and what time they appear in the video, in the description box for easy access to information.

The Neverending Queer-y: My Queer Ace Journey by Vesper (Queer as Cat): http://bit.do/The-Neverending-Queery
In this video, Vesper goes back through old YouTube videos and uses them to document the last decade of their journey with gender and sexuality. It includes a look at changing labels, evolving identities and the ongoing process of figuring stuff out.

How I Knew I Was Transgender by Jammidodger: http://bit.do/How-I-Knew-I-Was-Transgender

Gender Dysphoria Before & After Transitioning by Jammidodger: http://bit.do/Gender-Dysphoria

Just Gender Dysphoria Things by Jammidodger: http://bit.do/Just-Gender-Dysphoria-Things
In these videos, Jamie talks about how he figured out that he is transgender, and also goes into more detail about the ways that gender dysphoria can be experienced.

My Genderation Documentary Films by My Genderation: http://bit.do/My-Genderation
A playlist of short documentaries by trans filmmaking project My Genderation featuring a number of different trans people, of all ages and identities, talking about their lives and their experiences.

CHAPTER 4

Coming Out

Once you've figured out your own sexuality or gender identity, the next step you take may be to tell the people around you (friends, family and others). In the LGBTQIA+ community, this is called 'coming out'.

It's important to know that you don't *have* to come out as soon as you have figured out your sexuality or gender identity. You are not a bad person if you don't come out. You aren't letting anybody down. You should do what is best for you. That may mean waiting until you're safer or more independent before coming out. And that's okay.

Coming out can be a difficult thing for everybody. It can be particularly difficult for autistic people, as we can struggle to express or communicate our feelings with other people. In this chapter, we'll look at everything to do with coming out – the different things you can say, the different reactions people may have and how to respond to them, and, most importantly, how to stay safe when you do come out.

A lot of people think of coming out as a one-time thing but, in reality, it can be an ongoing thing that continues throughout your life.

For example, I came out to some of my friends first, then to my parents, and then my grandparents on one side of my family several years later. My grandparents on the other side died without knowing my sexuality (a choice that I made). I have still, despite being in my late twenties and living a very open life, not come out to some people in my family.

Luckily, as I am open about my sexuality on social media, I have avoided having to come out in person to many people. But social media can also be a problem for some people. Due to the very public nature of social media, it's important to be safe. This can mean that someone is forced to remain in the closet online or is forced to come out before they feel comfortable doing so.

Other than family and friends, there are other people that you may want to think about coming out to. For example, every time I have changed jobs, I have had to consider whether I need to come out to my new colleagues. At times, I have been very open with them straightaway. At other times, I have not mentioned it, or tried to drip-feed information rather than saying it. I found that the longer it went on without saying it, the harder it became to do so.

But this is my experience. My experience may not be your experience.

Not everybody is able to come out safely. There is no shame in not being able to come out. Nobody should be forced to come out, and nobody should be 'outed' (when people tell someone your sexuality or gender identity without your permission). Everybody's coming out story is different, and you must do what is best and safe for you.

Am I ready to come out?

Like with figuring out your sexuality and gender identity, there's unfortunately no way for anyone to definitively say whether you are ready to come out. Some people may never feel ready to come out, but will still do so in order to move their lives forward.

If you feel that you have figured out your sexuality or gender identity, and that you have had some time to accept this in yourself, then this may mean that you are ready to come out to others. Not coming out can be incredibly stressful. Knowing who you are but not being able to share that with the people around you can be damaging to your mental health.

As autistic people, we often spend a lot of time and effort trying to suppress our natural instincts. Whether it be holding in our stimming, forcing ourselves to make eye contact, or learning scripts for social situations, it can take a lot of emotional energy to be seen by outsiders as 'functioning'. Many autistic people call this 'masking', and it can be linked to high levels of depression and anxiety in the autistic community.

This 'masking' could be seen as very similar to being 'closeted'.

This is something that you have to weigh up against how comfortable you are in coming out, and how safe it is for you to come out. If being 'closeted' is hurting you, but you don't know if it's the right time to come out, it might be really helpful if you can speak to a trusted friend in confidence.

This might be someone that you know online or anonymously (you can find out more about making friends and staying safe online in Chapter 8). They might be able to help you work things out.

Even if you are still questioning your sexuality and gender identity, you may want to come out in order to gain support as you figure it out. You don't have to be absolutely certain in your identity in order to talk about it. It's fine to tell people 'I don't think I'm straight/cisgender, but I don't know what I am yet'. In fact, this may be really helpful in finding help and support in order to figure yourself out.

If you're unsure, or anxious, about whether you should come out, there are some organizations you can get in touch with (by phone, email, text or live chat) at the end of the chapter.

Is it safe for me to come out?

This is a really important question to ask yourself.

You will see a lot of people talking about the benefits of coming out. They are right, and there are a lot of benefits but, at the same time, it's important to make sure that you are safe.

This section isn't meant to scare you but it is important to do a risk assessment of the people around you before you come out.

While most of you will probably be in no danger when you come out, some family and friends are, unfortunately, not as tolerant or understanding as other people. If you don't think your family or friends will react well to you coming out, it's important to think about how you will handle the situation. If you are living at home, and know that your parents aren't accepting of LGBTQIA+ people, then make sure you have a back-up plan if coming out doesn't go well. Here are some ways that you can do this:

- Have a person (or people) you trust with you when you come out.
- Arrange a place to stay (this may be with a friend, or a more accepting family member) before coming out (so that you have somewhere to go if your home isn't safe).
- If you have a job, save up enough money before you come out so that you can move out and support yourself.
- If you have any savings accounts already (e.g. some people have accounts set up by their family for things like university or buying a house), make sure that you have access to this money before coming out. This might mean withdrawing it, or moving it to an account that is only in your name.
- Have a bag of essentials (clothes, toiletries, money, important documents like driving licence and passport, any stim toys you need, medications etc.) ready in case you need to leave home quickly.
- If you don't have anyone you can stay with, there are some organizations that can help, listed under 'Places to stay' in the 'More information' section at the end of the chapter.

Most of you will probably not need to do any of this.

If you are unsure how your family will react, and whether or not you need to do some of the above, it might be worth testing out how they might respond:

- Recommend a TV show or film that you know has LGBTQIA+ characters in it, and see how they react when watching it.
- Mention a prominent figure that is openly LGBTQIA+, and see how they react when talking about them.
- Mention a news story that you saw with an LGBTQIA+ theme (PinkNews may be a good resource to find one) and ask them what they think about it.

If you have a friend or family member whom you have already come out to and whom you trust, it can be helpful to get their opinion on how they think your family may react. If they are happy to do so, ask if they can do some of the 'testing out' tasks while your parents are around.

It might be best if this person is not autistic, as they may be more able to interpret your family's reaction.

If you need further advice and support from people with experience, but don't have anyone close to you, Switchboard LGBT+ is available to speak with you (or message/email you). You can find out more at: https://switchboard.lgbt.

Ways to come out

If you feel ready to come out, and are sure that it is safe to do so (or, if it isn't safe, are sure that you have some of the previously mentioned things in place to keep your safe) there are a lot of different ways that you can do it.

For most people, it's a case of sitting your family or friends down and directly telling them. This may be the most comfortable thing for some autistic people. However, direct conversations can also be difficult for a lot of autistic people, so it's important to remember that there are other ways to do it. This may involve asking someone you trust to do it for you (my mum told my grandparents on my request), or writing it in an email or letter.

Face to face
If you have decided to come out by talking to family and friends, it's good to think about how to start the conversation. This can be very awkward, so it might make you feel more comfortable to plan what you're going to say beforehand.

You can start the conversation by saying, 'Hi, would it be okay to sit down for a quick chat?' You can also do this by texting, emailing or leaving a note to let them know that you would like to have a chat. You might also want to add 'don't worry, it's nothing bad' to stop the other person being too tense or nervous (as this might make it more difficult for you).

When you have the person in the room, there are lots of different ways that you can tell them. It may be best to say it straightaway, and writing a script beforehand can help you to be more confident with what you have to say: 'Thank you for coming to have a chat with me. I just wanted to tell you that I'm [here you say the sexuality or gender identity that you are coming out as].'

You can edit this to work better for you. It may be helpful to add in 'I love you' at the beginning, depending on your relationship with the person, or to say something like, 'I've been thinking about this for a really long time and I want to tell you...' (letting them know that this isn't something that has come out of the blue, or that you haven't thought through).

It may also be a good idea to have a script ready for any

questions they might have. We'll go through these potential questions in a little while.

If you aren't certain that you will be safe to come out, make sure you have someone with you whom you trust. You can also have someone else with you for support, even if you do feel safe to come out. It can be helpful to discuss your script with this person beforehand, so that if you struggle to actually say the words, you can give them permission or a pre-agreed signal to do it for you (this is what happened when I came out to my grandparents – I couldn't get the words out, so I gave my mum an agreed signal for her to say it for me). If you need someone else to say it for you, it doesn't mean that you are weak or that you aren't brave. You are brave for coming out, however you do it, and you should always do what's best for you in the situation.

Alternatively, it may be safer for you not to come out in a face-to-face discussion at all. We'll look at the alternative options next.

In writing
If you can't come out face to face, or if you're not sure if it's safe to do so, writing it down can be the best way to come out. There are several ways that you can do this:

- A letter – writing it down by hand on a piece of paper can be a really personal way of coming out, and this can feel more intimate for you and for the person you are coming out to. Alternatively, you may prefer to write it out on the computer and then print it out. Once you have the letter written, you may want to leave it somewhere where the person will find it (by the side of their bed or in their bag), or post it through their door by hand, or even send it by post. Sending it by post may be the least stressful, as it takes it completely out of your hands.

- An email – this is the more 'modern' version of sending a letter in the post, so it might be more comfortable for you. Like sending a letter in the post, it might be less stressful as, once the email is sent, it takes the action out of your hands. As it goes directly to the person, you can be sure that it won't get lost or be accidentally picked up by somebody else. You have the option of just writing 'I'm [here is where you say the sexuality or gender identity that you are coming out as]' as the title, so they can immediately see it in their inbox, or you can write it in the main text of the email, meaning they wouldn't be able to read it unless they opened the email.

- A text/chat message (Facebook Chat, WhatsApp etc.) – again, this is a more 'modern' version of sending a letter in the post, so it may be something that you feel more comfortable doing. A text is something that you can write very quickly. It's very informal, so may be less stressful than having to sit down and write out a letter or an email. If it's something that you do a lot in your everyday life, as many of us do, then you may find this an easier option. However, as it is an immediate way to communicate, the response may also be immediate from the person you are coming out to. If you need time to breathe after sending the message, it may be worth turning off notifications on your phone or putting your phone on 'airplane' mode so you don't get the response until you feel ready.

If you struggle with writing, particularly if you have dyslexia (as many autistic people do), it may be worth bringing in a trusted person (whom you are already out to) to translate what you want to say into the format you want to use.

I know that we've painted a pretty bleak picture here, in that we've focused on what to do if coming out is unsafe for you. This is important, as it will apply to some people, and I want those people to be safe. However, for many people, coming out won't be something that's so risky as to need a back-up plan. That doesn't mean it isn't scary, but you may want to deal with that fear by doing something a little bit more interesting or fun.

Mixing it up
If you are safe, and have a family that you are certain will accept you, you may want to think about more interesting and quirky ways to come out. Not only can this be a lot of fun for you and anyone helping you, but it can also help to lessen any tension and create a more light-hearted environment for everyone involved (particularly you and the people you are coming out to).

Here are some fun ways that people have come out to their families:

- Baking a cake – there have been several viral photos of people who have baked a cake and piped their coming out message on the top before giving it to their family/ friends.
- Make a card – this can be particularly fun if you're coming out as a different gender to the one assigned to you at birth (e.g. an 'it's a girl!' or 'it's a boy!' card).
- Put an announcement in the paper – another one that

can be fun if coming out as a different gender to the one assigned to you at birth, this is often done by parents or family members rather than the person themselves (with permission from the person, of course). There have been quite a few viral stories of parents announcing their 'new' son or daughter in the newspaper (often referring to there having been a mistake for the previous however many years, and how proud they are). This is obviously something to do after you have come out to your parents, and should be thought about very carefully.

- Throwing a party – you can throw a surprise 'coming out' party and invite the people you want to come out to. You could decorate the room with rainbows, bake a cake (see one of the previous suggestions) and surprise the people you are coming out to when they arrive (this could be with a banner, a cake, a song or anything else you can think of).
- Playing a game – YouTuber Elle Mills came out as bisexual to her friends by describing her crush and getting them to draw what they thought the person looked like on camera. She then handed them a picture of her crush, revealing that it was a woman and that she was attracted to women. She also came out to her family by decorating the front of her house to make it look like a rainbow. There is a link to this video at the end of the chapter.

These are just a few suggestions of fun ways that you can come out. It can also be fun to sit down and think of other ways with people you trust.

Just make sure that you are safe, and that the people you

trust agree that you are safe, before you think about coming out in one of these ways.

How might they react

Saying the words, or making the initial statement, is very important and you should be proud of yourself for getting through that bit, but be aware that this is just the beginning of coming out.

The person you are coming out to will probably want to talk, and it's very likely that they will have questions. It might be a good idea for you to prepare some answers to those questions, and to put together a script for yourself to respond to some of the reactions that you might get. Here are some ideas.

'Are you sure?'
Yes, I've thought about this a lot, and I am sure. I am sure that I am [your sexuality or gender identity] in the same way that you are sure that you are [their sexuality or gender identity].

'Are you just confused?'
No, I'm not confused. I've done a lot of work to figure this out, and I'm less confused now than I was before I realized that I'm [your sexuality or gender identity].

'Why are you doing this?'
It's not a thing that I'm doing, it's just who I am. I'm not telling you to hurt you, but because I want to be completely honest with you.

'Maybe you haven't met the right person?'
This is about who I am, not who I'm dating. Did you know you were

[their sexuality] before you met the 'right person'? Well, it's the same for me.

'Maybe you're just a tomboy/feminine boy?'
I've thought about it a lot, and it's definitely more than that. I would still be [your gender identity] even if I liked [stereotypical things for the sex you were assigned at birth]. This is who I am.

One of the main negative, or disbelieving, responses that you might get is this: 'You can't be [sexuality or gender identity] because you're autistic.' Some people can be very ignorant about this, and don't understand that autistic people can have sexual or romantic feelings or have an understanding of their own gender. You may want to respond with something like this:
Actually, a lot of autistic people are LGBTQIA+. There have been studies on this, and we're more likely to identify as something other than straight or cisgender than non-autistic people. Just because I'm autistic, doesn't mean I don't understand who I am. I know that I am [your sexuality or gender identity]. There is some more information under 'Autistic and LGBTQIA+' in the 'More information' section at the end of the chapter.

They may not understand straightaway. In this case, it's a good idea to give them these resources and walk away, allowing them the space to read about the topic and (it is hoped) come to an understanding. Let them know if you are happy to answer any questions they have. Maybe ask them to write them down so you can think about your answers before you reply.

You can also direct them to get in touch with FFLAG (Families and Friends of Lesbians and Gays), which offers support and information for families and friends of people who are LGBTQIA+: www.fflag.org.uk.

Is that it?

As we said right at the beginning of this chapter, coming out is very rarely a one-time thing. Once you have come out to the people who are most important to you (family, friends etc.), then you have cleared the hardest part. However, there will still be moments where you will have to make a decision on whether or not you should come out.

New friends

When making new friends, it's a good idea to tell them sooner rather than later. It can be difficult if you start to make a good friend, only for them to react badly when/if they find out. It's probably best not to make it the *first* thing you say, but you can mention it once you're a little way into chatting with them. If they say something that makes you think that they are not understanding of LGBTQIA+ people *before* you mention it, it's a good idea to step away from them or maybe ask an existing friend to help you.

New relationships

When you are interested in someone romantically, it's also a good idea to tell them sooner rather than later. This is particularly true if you like someone, or have begun dating someone, who doesn't identify as LGBTQIA+. It's good to be honest from the start. It's also a good test of whether they are going to accept who you are in a relationship. If they don't react well, then it's better to find out before you're too deeply involved in the relationship. If they say something that makes you think that they are not understanding of LGBTQIA+ people *before* you mention it, then again, it's a good idea to step away from them or maybe ask a friend to help you.

Note: this might be particularly challenging if you are trans and you are coming out to someone who is cis (particularly a straight cis man). There have been cases where straight, cis men have attacked trans women after finding out that they are trans. It's a good idea to use some of the techniques above (such as showing them a story about a trans person or talking about a person who is openly trans, and seeing what they think) to check and see if you are safe to come out.

New job
This one can be trickier, because you *have* to work with your colleagues whether they are understanding or not. You may want to get to know your new colleagues a little bit better before judging whether it's okay to tell them. You can use some of the techniques we explored earlier to test out how they might react to finding out. If you think they will be okay, the best way to tell them is to casually drop it into conversation (talking about a relationship you've had, or an event that you went to, or a group that you were a part of etc.).

If it's comfortable and safe for you to be honest, it's often a good idea to talk to your colleagues as soon as possible! Things were very awkward for me in a previous job: they all worked out pretty quickly that I wasn't straight, but they made the assumption that I was a lesbian. It wasn't until I was interviewed on a national news programme about bisexuality that they realized I wasn't actually a lesbian!

Doctors

This is something that might come up at any point in your life and so it's important to be prepared. It may be as simple as a nurse presuming you are dating someone of the opposite sex, or it may be a medical professional assuming that you have certain genitalia because of your gender. In these circumstances, it will probably be necessary for you to come out.

If you are dating someone of the same gender, you will need to make the medical professionals aware so that they can be properly treated as your significant other (particularly when discussing important medical decisions). If you are trans, you will need to come out to your doctor as your organs and genitalia might not be what they think they are. For example, if you are a woman with a penis (or a woman who has had a vaginoplasty), you may receive letters advising that you need a smear, and if you are a man with a cervix, you may *not* receive these letters. As it's important that any person with a cervix has their smear tests (as a way to detect and treat cervical cancer), you should make sure your doctor knows that you have a cervix. This means you will have to come out.

If a medical professional (or someone who works in your local surgery) reacts negatively or doesn't treat you correctly after you come out, it's a good idea to keep a note of everything that happens (including the people you have spoken to) and lodge a complaint with the surgery. If you're unhappy with the response, or don't want to complain directly to the surgery, you can complain to your local NHS services or your local NHS ombudsman.

There is more information about lodging a complaint on the Which website: www.which.co.uk/consumer-rights/advice/how-to-complain-if-youre-unhappy-with-your-gp-or-gp-surgery.

You can get support for your complaint at your local Health-watch: www.healthwatch.co.uk/your-local-healthwatch/list.

Note: If you are a person with a vagina who has only had sex with other people with vaginas, your doctor may tell you that you don't need a smear test. This is incorrect. If you want one (bearing in mind that it is a good idea to have one, but it is your decision) let the doctor know that you still need one. If they refuse, please follow the complaints procedure to appeal the decision.

The most important thing

Your safety is the most important thing. It can be very difficult to keep a secret this big, but if it's needed to keep you safe then you need to try. If you are worried about how your family will react to you coming out, make sure you are financially stable and/or have a back-up plan (such as a friend or family member to stay with) before you come out. If you need to speak to someone about it, or need some advice, you can contact one of the organizations under 'Safety' in the 'More information' section below (all of which have non-phone options).

More information

Books

Gender Identity, Sexuality and Autism by Eva A. Mendes and Meredith R. Maroney

Trans Teen Survival Guide by Owl and Fox Fisher

LGBTQ: The Survival Guide for Lesbian, Gay, Bisexual, Transgender, and Questioning Teens by Kelly Huegel Madrone

The Pride Guide: A Guide to Sexual and Social Health for LGBTQ Youth
by Jo Langford

Links

Gendered Intelligence: http://genderedintelligence.co.uk/projects/
kip/comingout

YouTube videos

These are some coming out videos (or videos about coming out) that I have seen, and that have had an impact on me. There are lots of these videos on the internet – you can search 'coming out' for more.

Basically I'm Gay by Daniel Howell: http://bit.do/Basically-Im-Gay
In this video, Dan talks about the journey to figuring out his sexuality, his relationship with different labels and how he got to where he is now.

Coming Out (Elle Mills Style) by Elle Mills: http://bit.do/Coming-Out-Elle-Mills
Elle comes out as bisexual to her friends by getting them to guess who she has a crush on and then revealing that it's a woman. She then decorates the outside of her house in rainbow colours in order to come out to her family.

I'm Gay by Eugene Lee Yang: http://bit.do/Im-Gay-Eugene
Eugene comes out in a beautifully shot and choreographed music video detailing his journey.

Coming Out as Transgender to my Sisters In-Law by Jammidodger:
http://bit.do/Coming-Out-As-Trans

Ways to Come Out as Transgender by Jammidodger: http://bit.do/
Ways-To-Come-Out-As-Transgender
In the first video, Jamie and his fiancée, Shaaba, tell Shaaba's young
sisters that Jamie is transgender, what that means, and answer any
questions they have. It's lovely. In the second video, Jamie looks at
fun ways to come out as trans.

The Sex Education You Never Had *PRIDE EDITION* by Ellbat: http://
bit.do/Sex-Education-You-Never-Had
In this hour-long video, Ellbat (with an appearance by Fox Fisher)
answers lots of questions about all things LGBTQIA+, including
how to come out as trans to your family. You can find the questions
you need answering, and what time they appear in the video, in
the description box for easy access to information.

Places to stay

AKT (formerly The Albert Kennedy Trust) – An organization specifically
designed to combat LGBTQIA+ homelessness

Phone:
- If you're in the South, call the London office: 020 7831 6562
- If you're in the North West, call the Manchester office: 0161 228 3308
- If you're in the North East, call the Newcastle office: 0191 281 0099
- If you're not in any of these areas, you can call the one nearest to you or
  contact them online

Online support (lets you speak to a digital mentor):
- www.akt.org.uk/online-support

For more information on getting support from AKT:
- www.akt.org.uk/refer

Nightstop – An organization that tries to prevent homelessness in young
people through community hosting

Phone:
- 020 7939 1220

Finding local support:
- www.nightstop.org.uk/contact-us

The Runaway Helpline – An organization to support people who have run away, or who are thinking of running away

Phone:
- 116 000 (free call or text)

Email:
- 116000@runawayhelpline.org.uk

Online chat:
- www.runawayhelpline.org.uk (chat box is on the bottom right of each page of the website)

Shelter – An organization offering support and advice on all aspects of housing

Phone:
- England: 0808 800 4444 (8am to 8pm on weekdays, 9am to 5pm on weekends)
- Scotland: 0808 800 4444 (9am to 5pm on weekdays)
- Wales: 0345 075 5005 (9.30am to 4.00pm on weekdays only, you can ask for a Welsh speaking service)

Online support:
- England: https://england.shelter.org.uk/get_help/webchat (online chat service, 9am to 5pm on weekdays only)
- Scotland: https://scotland.shelter.org.uk/about_us/contact_us
- Wales: https://sheltercymru.org.uk/email-advice (fill in the online form)

Face-to-face support:
- England: https://england.shelter.org.uk/get_help/local_services (put in your postcode to find a local service)
- Scotland: https://scotland.shelter.org.uk/about_us/projects
- Wales: https://sheltercymru.org.uk/get-advice/advice-near-you

Other useful numbers –
Citizens Advice Bureau: 03444 111 444
Samaritans: 116 123
National LGBT Domestic Violence Helpline: 0300 999 5428/0800 999 5428
Switchboard LGBT+: 0300 330 0630

Autistic and LGBTQIA+
Twainbow

A support group for autistic LGBTQIA+ people, with information and resources on their website (www.twainbow.org).

Gender Identity, Sexuality and Autism by Eva A. Mendes and Meredith R. Maroney

A book bringing together a collection of narratives from people who identify as LGBTQIA+ and autistic (www.jkp.com/uk/gender-identity-sexuality-and-autism-2.html).

Under A Double Rainbow: Autism and LGBTQIA+ by Maxfield Sparrow

An article about people who are autistic and LGBTQIA+, including resources, tips for parents/carers and personal experiences (www.thinkingautismguide.com/2017/11/under-double-rainbow-autism-and-lgbtqia.html).

Safety

Stonewall – A campaigning organization for the equality of LGBT people across Britain:

Online information service:

- www.stonewall.org.uk/help-advice/contact-stonewalls-information-service

Advice on coming out:

- www.stonewall.org.uk/help-advice/coming-out/coming-out-young-person

Switchboard – An LGBTQIA+ specific helpline

Phone:

- 0300 330 0630 (open 10am to 10pm every day)

Live chat:

- https://switchboard.lgbt/# (click the purple speech bubble at the bottom right-hand corner to activate the live chat)

Mermaids – An organization offering support to young people who are trans, gender variant, or questioning their gender:

Phone:

- 0808 801 0400 (open 9am to 9pm Monday to Friday, although bank holidays may vary. If you can't get through, leave a message with your phone number and they will call you back. If you have a specific time when you would prefer someone to call back, say this in the message you leave)

Email:

- info@mermaidsuk.org.uk

Online chat:

- https://mermaidsuk.org.uk/contact-us (the chat box is on the bottom right of this page. Click the 'Let's Chat' button. If the chat option isn't available, the button will say 'Sorry our web chat is currently closed')

Youth forum:

- https://mermaidsuk.org.uk/young-people/youth-forum (an online safe space to speak to other young people who may have gone through the same thing)
- You will have to complete a form (with a valid email address) and request to join the forum. You may want to set up a new email address for this if it's safer for you

Childline – A counselling service for children and young people in the UK provided by the NSPCC:

Phone:

- 0800 1111 (free and open 24/7, although calls between midnight and 7.30am may be limited to 15 minutes)
- There are some Welsh-speaking counsellors. When calling, let them know that you would like to speak to someone in Welsh and a time will be arranged for you to do this

Online chat:

- www.childline.org.uk/get-support/1-2-1-counsellor-chat (click the box on the right-hand side to enter the waiting room. There is a traffic light system to indicate how busy the service is, and how long you might have to wait)

Art box:

- www.childline.org.uk/toolbox/art-box (this enables you to draw about how you are feeling. If you struggle to express yourself with words, or English isn't your first language, you can share what you draw with the counsellor you speak to in the online chat)
- You will need to create an account and sign in to save what you draw. You can do this by clicking on the box in the bottom right-hand corner next to the Art box

Message boards:

- www.childline.org.uk/get-support/message-boards (you can chat with other young people who understand or may have gone through the same thing

Advice on coming out:

- www.childline.org.uk/info-advice/your-feelings/sexual-identity/ coming-out

CHAPTER 5

Transitioning

Note: this chapter will look at the process of transitioning to your correct gender identity. If you are cisgender (your gender matches the gender you were assigned at birth), you are welcome to skip to the next chapter. However, reading this might be helpful to understand what your trans friends are experiencing (and how you can support them).

If you are trans, the next step after coming out may be to transition. Transition means to begin living as your correct gender identity. This may include changing your name, changing your pronouns, changing your appearance, updating your professional documents (like your passport or driver's licence), or pursuing medical treatment (like hormones or gender confirmation surgery).

There isn't one correct way to transition. Your transition will depend on what works best for you. It's also important to remember you should only transition if it's safe to do so.

Some people only present as their correct gender in certain circumstances – for example, presenting with their chosen name, pronouns and gender among friends or on social media, while remaining in the closet (presenting as cisgender) when they're around their family or in school/the workplace.

This chapter will explore two different aspects of transitioning: social transitioning and medical transitioning. It will provide information on different things that you can do to help your transition, how to safely access those things, and how to advocate for yourself if you need medical help.

Before that, however, we'll look at gender identity clinics: what they are, how to get a referral, and how to navigate them as an autistic person (as many gender identity clinics don't have specific training regarding trans autistic patients).

Gender identity clinics

What are they?
While trans people and people questioning their gender have mostly the same health needs as cis people, there are some specific things that a regular doctor can't do, such as provide support for those questioning their gender or experiencing gender dysphoria, and give access to medical treatments like hormones and gender confirmation surgery.

That's what gender identity clinics (GICs) are there for – to meet the specific health needs of trans people. They are also there to meet the specific health needs of people who are questioning their gender or aren't sure if they are trans.

If you need medical treatment as part of your transition, you will need to get a referral to a GIC.

However, if you do not want any medical treatment as part of your transition, you can still attend a GIC for advice and support. If you aren't sure if you want medical treatment, or aren't sure if you are trans at all, it's worth attending a GIC to look at your options and find the support you need to make any later decisions.

How do I get a referral?
You get a referral to a GIC through your GP.

Book an appointment with your GP, and take a trusted person (e.g. parent, friend, other family member) with you if you can. Before the appointment, it's helpful to make a note of all the reasons why you need to be referred to a GIC – this might include how you're feeling, articles or books that you've read and relate to, what you feel about your gender, and specifically what you need. This can be helpful if you become anxious or struggle to talk or remember things during the appointment.

When the doctor asks why you are there, say, 'I think I am transgender, and I need to be referred to a gender identity clinic.' This lets them know exactly what is going on, and outlines exactly what you think needs to happen.

If they ask any more questions, this is when your notes may come in handy. You might also want to give permission for the person accompanying you to speak on your behalf. Make sure you discuss or share notes with this person before the appointment.

What if they won't refer me?
If your doctor won't refer you to a GIC, you are allowed to ask to see another doctor. This might mean seeing another doctor in the practice. It might also mean leaving your doctor and signing up to another practice. If you need to do this, make sure that there are spaces available at another practice

before leaving your current one – you don't want to be left without a doctor!

Are GICs autism trained?

GIC staff may not have had specific autism training. They might not understand that you can be autistic and trans, or they might assume that you're confused or can't make decisions this big by yourself. It is hoped that this won't happen, but some autistic trans people have reported having this experience. It's important to make sure you are prepared for this when you get your appointment.

Here are some things that you can do:

- Make sure that you let them know you're autistic before the appointment.
- Write down a list of your specific needs (including how best to communicate with you, whether you may need a longer appointment, that you need to record the appointment for future reference etc.).
- Take an appropriate adult or advocate with you (if you have one).
- Take with you some information on autism, as they may have misconceptions or believe common myths that may sway their opinion. Some information you may want to take with you can be found under 'Information on autism' in the 'More information' section at the end of this chapter.

How long is the waiting list?

Once your doctor refers you, it's important to remember that you won't get a GIC appointment immediately. The waiting list could be up to a couple of years.

This can be really difficult, so you might want to look for help and support while you're waiting. This could be from your friends, or it could be from an organization like Mermaids or Gendered Intelligence. We'll include links to these organizations at the end of the chapter.

If the waiting list is too long, you may want to look into attending a private clinic. This can be expensive, but more and more people are choosing to go down this route to avoid the distressing waiting times at NHS clinics.

If you decide that you would like to go private, and you can afford it, do your research to make sure you are seeing someone who is fully qualified. You deserve the best service from the best people, so don't just go to the first one you find. You can ask your family doctor to check the credentials of any private specialists you find.

You might also want to look for information and support from organizations like Mermaids and Gendered Intelligence when it comes to finding a good private clinic.

You don't have to wait for your GIC appointment in order to start your *social transition*.

Social transition

When you socially transition, it means you begin to transition from living as your assigned sex to living as the gender that you have realized you are. It might mean changing your clothes, cutting/growing your hair, changing your name and pronouns (and asking people to refer to you using your chosen name and pronouns), using binders and other devices to modify your appearance, and anything else that you feel you need to do.

Socially transitioning is different from medically transi

tioning, as there is usually no surgery or medication involved (medically transitioning involves taking hormones or having surgery). Not everyone who transitions wants to medically transition – if you feel happy with just your social transition, this is fine. If you do want to transition medically, then socially transitioning is often the first step towards this.

We'll have a closer look at medically transitioning a little bit later in the chapter. Now, we'll look at some of the things you may do as part of your social transition, and how you can do them.

Changing your pronouns

One of the first things you might want to do is to try changing your pronouns.

A pronoun is the word that people use when they are talking about you, but don't use your name.

For example:
'Erin's at the door, *she* has brought *her* mum with *her*'.
'Have you seen *his* new film?'
'Someone left *their* hat in my house last night.'

Pronouns are traditionally understood to be masculine (he, him, his), feminine (she, her, hers) and plural, when talking about more than one person (they, them, theirs). So-called 'plural' pronouns are also traditionally used when the gender of the person you're talking about is unknown (for example, as we don't know *who* left the hat at my house, we use 'their' instead of 'his' or 'her').

Just because this is how they are traditionally used does not mean that you have to use them this way. You are welcome to use whichever pronouns you prefer.

Although many trans women use 'she/her' pronouns, and many trans men prefer 'he/him' pronouns, and many non-binary people prefer 'they/them' pronouns, you do not have to use these pronouns if you don't want to.

There are also alternative pronouns, or 'neopronouns' that some people prefer to use (which we'll look at a little bit later).

Changing your pronouns can be a very important first step in your social transition.

Some pronouns to try
Traditional gendered pronouns
He/him/his/himself – traditionally 'male' pronouns
She/her/hers/herself – traditionally 'female' pronouns

Traditional gender neutral pronouns
They/them/their/themselves – traditionally plural (referring to more than one person) and gender neutral pronouns
It/it/its/itself – traditional gender neutral pronoun commonly used for objects, animals and infants. While it is often seen as insulting to use these for another person, some non-binary people like to use 'it' pronouns.

Neopronouns
Neopronouns are gender neutral pronouns that are different from traditional pronouns (such as he, she, they and it).
Xe/xir/xirs/xirself – gender neutral neopronouns, first recorded use was in the 1990s.
Xe/xyr or xem/xyrs/xyrself or xemself – gender neutral neopronouns, first used as an option on an autism mailing list in the 1990s.
Ze/hir/hirs/hirself – gender neutral neopronouns, first recorded use was in the late 1990s and early 2000s. They have been used in several fantasy and science fiction stories.

Zie/zir or zim/zirs/zirself – gender neutral neopronouns, first recorded use was in the late 1990s and early 2000s. They have been used in several fantasy and science fiction stories. E/em/eir/eirs/emself – gender neutral neopronoun, first recorded use in the 1990s.

Nounself pronouns

Nounself pronouns are when you adapt a noun of your choosing into a pronoun to create a wide variety of very personal and descriptive pronouns.

Fae/faer/faers/faerself – fairy-themed gender-neutral nounself pronoun. First recorded use was online in the 2010s.

What should I change my pronouns to?

Some people know immediately which pronouns they identify with. If you have realized that you are a woman, or have recently come out as being a woman, you may know straightaway that you want people to use she/her pronouns.

For other people, it can help to experiment with different pronouns. If you have realized that you are neither a man nor a woman, then it may take you a little bit of trial and error before you find which pronouns you prefer.

In the 2019 Gender Census, the most popular gender neutral pronouns were:

- They/them (79.5%)
- Xe/xem (7.2%)
- E/em (5.2%)
- Ze/hir (4.7%)
- It/its (4.4%)
- Fae/faer (4.3%)

The website nonbinary.wiki suggests a series of steps when deciding which pronouns to use:

1. Set up a list of what you're looking for in a pronoun, and then number the points in order of importance. Here are some examples of criteria you might look at:
   - Used by many real people
   - Pronounceable, easy to say out loud
   - Easy to spell
   - Accessible, easy for people to use who have trouble with English
   - Sound like a mix of 'she' and 'he' pronouns
   - Don't sound at all like 'she' or 'he', to get more distance from the gender binary
   - Sound like standard English pronouns, but with a twist
   - Symbolic, describing you or your gender
   - Liked by your friends and family
   - Good for people who are strict about grammar
   - Make it easy to persuade other people that it's okay to use these pronouns for you

2. If more than one pronoun passes your list of criteria, set up a table of 'pros' (reasons to use them) and 'cons' (reasons not to use them):

Pronoun	Pros	Cons	Conclusion
ve, verself	Used in a book I like	Doesn't sound right to me	Maybe no
E, Emself	Common, easy to say	Too short?	Maybe yes

3. Test any pronouns you like:
   - Write them down
   - Say them out loud
   - Ask any trusted friends and family to say them out loud when referring to you.

4. Remember that what you liked in theory might not fit you so well in practice, so keep trying until you find one you like and are comfortable with.

Some people prefer to use multiple pronouns. For example, some people are comfortable using 'they/them' pronouns and 'he/him' pronouns. People who are gender fluid may prefer different pronouns on different occasions.

Remember, you are allowed to change your mind later on. You might feel a bit different a few months or years from now. That's okay.

The best way to see if your new chosen pronouns work for you is to start using them in your everyday life.

Using your new pronouns
Once you've decided on your new pronouns, you will probably want to start using them. Doing this may give you a better idea whether these are *definitely* the right pronouns for you. Just because you've started using your pronouns doesn't mean you can't change them in the future – see how you feel, what it's like to be referred to with these pronouns, and then do what feels best for you.

The first thing to do is to speak to the people closest to you (whom you trust) and ask that they start referring to you by your new pronouns. This might include family, friends, close co-workers and online friends. Let them know what your pronouns are and how they work (e.g. if you are using neopronouns, people might need some help understanding how they work).

If you feel safe to, add your pronouns to your profile on whatever social media platforms you use. These could be in your profile biography, or they could be added as part of your username (e.g. my Twitter handle could be 'Erin Ekins (she/her)').

Twitter allows you to use a username rather than your real name, so this may be a good place to anonymously ask people to start using the correct pronouns. You don't have to add your full name, or display any personal details or pictures, so you can be as anonymous as you like. You can also make your tweets private, so people have to request to view them, and you can make sure they are safe.

When you are ready for people at work or school to start using your pronouns, ask for a meeting with your manager or teacher. Take a trusted friend or family member if you can. Write down what you want to say beforehand. Explain that you would like people to refer to you with different pronouns, and ask that they let your colleagues, other teachers or classmates know about the change.

If you have an email signature at work, it might be a good idea to speak to your manager about everyone including their pronouns in the signature. This means that people contacting you will know your pronouns, but also means you aren't singled out as the only person with their pronouns in their email signature.

If people accidentally use the wrong pronoun, it's important to correct them. This can be scary, but it is the only way to help them get used to it. They will probably appreciate being reminded, particularly if they've been referring to you one way for a long time.

A good way to remind them if they use the wrong pronoun is to just firmly, but politely, say your correct pronouns, accept any apology they give and move on with the conversation.

For people getting used to your new pronouns, it might help them (and you) to let them know how to correct themselves: apologize, correct the mistake, and move on.

If some of your friends refuse to change the pronouns they use to refer to you, have a chat with friends you trust and ask them to speak to them for you. If any of your friends still refuse to use the correct pronouns, it might be healthier for you to step back from being their friend.

If you go into a new environment, such as a new job, you may want to introduce yourself with your new pronouns: Hi, *my name is [your name], and my pronouns are [your pronouns]*. However, if you don't feel comfortable doing this, be aware that people may assume your pronouns and get them wrong.

Sharing your pronouns can be a form of coming out, so, as was said in the chapter on coming out, the priority is to make sure that you feel safe.

Changing your name

Another early step you might want to take is changing your name.

Not everybody who socially transitions wants to or needs to change their name. If you don't change your name, or can't change your name at the moment, it doesn't make you less trans than someone who does or can.

A lot of people, even cis people, change their name as part of moving on to a different part of their lives.

What should I change it to?
If you have realized that you are a woman, and you have a name that is more traditionally masculine, you may want to change your name to something more traditionally feminine. If you have realized that you're a man, and you have a name that is more traditionally feminine, you may want to change your name to something more traditionally masculine.

If you have realized that you are neither a man nor a woman, or that your gender is more fluid, you may want to change your name to something more traditionally gender neutral (names like Charlie, Chris, Sam, Jo and Alex can be popular).

You may even want to change your name to something that is a bit more unusual or uncommon. Some of the names that people I know have chosen include Taran, Valour and Raven.

Whatever you change your name to, it's a good idea to really think very hard about it. You want to choose something that you like, and something that you think suits you. It's useful to draw up a shortlist of names you like. You might want to discuss it with people you trust and who know you well (this may in person, or it may be online, depending on who your friends are and how you best communicate with them).

Before legally changing your name, it's a good idea to ask people to start using it. This is to get an idea of whether it's right for you.

You can use the same steps that you used when thinking about your pronouns when picking your name:

1. Set up a list of what you're looking for in a name, and then number the points in order of importance. Here are some examples of criteria you might look at:
   - Used by many real people
   - Pronounceable, easy to say out loud
   - Easy to spell
   - Accessible, easy for people to use who have trouble with English
   - Is a traditional, more common name
   - Is a less traditional, more unique name
   - Sounds like a standard English name, but with a twist
   - Symbolic, describes you or your personality
   - Your friends and family like it
   - Makes it easy to persuade other people that it's okay to use this name for you

2. If more than one name passes your list of criteria, set up a table of 'pros' (reasons to use them) and 'cons' (reasons not to use them):

Name	Pros	Cons	Conclusion
Tom	Simple, traditional	Doesn't sound right to me	Maybe no
Taran	More unique, but still simple	Will people use it?	Maybe yes

3. Test any names you like.
   - Write them down
   - Say them out loud
   - Ask any trusted friends and family to say them out loud when referring to you.

4. Remember that what you liked in theory might not fit you so well in practice, so keep trying until you find a name you like and are comfortable with.

Using your new name

Once you've decided on your new name, you will probably want to start using it. It's a good idea to do this before you change your name legally, to make sure that you like it.

The first thing to do is to speak to the people closest to you (whom you trust) and ask that they start calling you by your new name. This might include family, friends, close co-workers and online friends. Let them know what your new name is.

If you feel safe to, change your name on whatever social media you are on.

Facebook is probably the most common one, as it asks for you to use your name rather than a username.

If it isn't safe for you to let everyone know about your new name (e.g. if you're not out to your family), you might want to set up a separate Facebook page with your new name, and only invite the people you trust. Make sure you set the privacy settings to 'private' so people who aren't your friends can't see your posts. It's probably best not to use a picture of you as your profile picture, as people who are not friends will be able to see it.

Twitter allows you to use a username rather than your real name, so this may be a good place to anonymously ask people to start using your new name. You may want to put your new first name in your screen name, and ask people to refer to you by that name. You don't have to add your full name, or display any personal details or pictures, so you can be as anonymous as you like. You can also make your tweets private, so people have to request to view them, and you can make sure they are safe.

When you are ready for people at work or school to start using your new name, ask for a meeting with your manager or teacher. Take a trusted friend or family member if you can. Write down what you want to say beforehand. Explain that you would like people to call you by a different name, and ask that they let your colleagues, other teachers or classmates know about the change.

If people accidentally call you the wrong name, it's important to correct them. This can be scary, but it is the only way to help them get used to it. They will probably appreciate being reminded, particularly if they've known you as your previous name for a long time.

A good way to remind them if they use the wrong name is to just firmly, but politely, say your new name, accept any apology they give and move on with the conversation.

For people getting used to your new name, it might help them (and you) to let them know how to correct themselves: apologize, correct the mistake, and move on.

If some of your friends refuse to use your new name, have a chat with friends you trust and ask them to speak to them for you. If any of your friends still refuse to use your new name, it might be healthier for you to step back from being their friend.

If you go into a new environment, such as a new job, introduce yourself as your new name rather than your old one. This may be more difficult if you have not legally changed your name, as your legal name will appear on your official documents.

So, once you are confident and comfortable with your new name, the next step is to change your name legally.

Legally changing your name

You don't have to legally change your name before you start using your new name. However, in order to make sure you have the right name on your official documents (e.g. driver's licence, passport, bank account), you have to apply for a deed poll.

A deed poll is a legal document that says three things:

- I am abandoning my previous name.
- I will use my new name at all times.
- I require everyone to address me by my new name only.

There are two different types of deed poll:

- An 'unenrolled' deed poll – if you are 16 or over, you can change your name yourself. This involves downloading the correct forms, filling them in, and returning them.
- An 'enrolled' deed poll – this means you are putting your new name on public record, and you must be 18 or over to do this. It also costs money and is a longer process.

You do not have to enrol your deed poll in order for your name change to be legal.

If you do enrol your deed poll, the record of your name change will be held at the Royal Courts of Justice for five years, before being moved to an archive. Other than this, there is no real difference between an enrolled and an unenrolled deed poll.

Many people go with the unenrolled deed poll, because it

is quicker, cheaper and less complicated. It's estimated that only 1 in 200 people who change their name do it through enrolled deed poll.

The website www.legal-deedpolls.co.uk says this:

> There is no real benefit to enrolling your deed poll, apart from it being made a public record. A deed poll provides the exact same service as an enrolled deed poll, which is why they are so unpopular. (www.legal-deedpolls.co.uk/blog/enrolling-deed-poll)

If you choose to get an unenrolled deed poll, as most people do, there are two ways that you can do it.

You can make your own, by writing a document that says:

I [old name] of [your address] have given up my name [old name] and have adopted for all purposes the name [new name].

Signed as a deed on [date] as [old name] and [new name] in the presence of [witness 1 name] of [witness 1 address], and [witness 2 name] of [witness 2 address].

[your new signature], [your old signature]

[witness 1 signature], [witness 2 signature]

However, most people prefer to get professionals to write up this document for them. This is so that the document looks more official, and so it should be easier to get things like banks and the passport office to change their records. This can cost money, but should be less than you would pay for an enrolled deed poll. You can find companies that specialize in this by using an internet search engine such as Google.

Don't just go with the first organization you find. You have to find one that will do a good job. Have a look at review websites like Trustpilot.com before picking a professional service. If you have someone who can help you with this – a friend or a family member – this can help prevent you from accidentally going through a bad organization.

You can *also* change your title using the deed poll. For example, if you are a woman but have 'Mr' as your title on your records, you can change it to 'Ms', 'Miss' or 'Mrs' when you complete your deed poll. Speak to whichever professional you are using to write the deed poll about doing this.

If you have questions about changing your name, organizations like Mermaids, which supports young trans and gender diverse people, should be able to answer them or walk you through the process.

Changing your name on documents

Once you have your deed poll as proof that your name is legally changed, you can get your name changed on things like your passport, your bank accounts, your driving licence and other things.

The first thing to do is to sit down, by yourself or with someone you trust, and draw up a list of all the places where you'll need to officially change your name and how to get in touch with them. You can then tick them off as you go!

Here are some that you might want to think about:

- Bank accounts
- Passport
- Driving licence (or provisional driving licence)

- School records
- Medical records
- Department for Work and Pensions (covering National Insurance, benefits and pensions)
- Any outgoing payments that you have (car insurance, pet insurance, phone bill etc.).

Again, some of these places might require you to call them. If you have problems with phone calls, get a trusted person to make the call while you sit next to them. They might ask you to confirm that you are happy for this trusted person to speak for you, so you may have to answer some questions. Let them know you are autistic and you struggle with making calls, and answer their questions as best as you can. If you are non-verbal, you and your trusted person will need to make arrangements with the company about what to do.

For any bank accounts, you should be able to go into your local branch with your name change document and they will change the name on all of your accounts and set you up with any new cards.

For your passport, you will have to apply for a new passport under your new legal name. This will cost around £75, and you can make these changes online at www.gov.uk/changing-passport-information. You can change your photo when you do this, if you've altered your appearance.

For your driving licence, you will have to apply for a new licence, sending in your old licence and proof of your name change. You can change your photo when you do this, if you've altered your appearance slightly. Find out more here: www.gov.uk/change-name-driving-licence.

When it comes to changing your name with the Department for Work and Pensions, you will have to send proof of your legal name change, along with a covering letter and your National Insurance number (you will have automatically received a National Insurance card with your National Insurance number when you turned 16). The organization Gendered Intelligence has more information here: http://genderedintelligence.co.uk/projects/kip/transitioning/docs/depwork.

Gendered Intelligence has lots of other information on changing your name on documents here: http://genderedintelligence.co.uk/projects/kip/transitioning/docs.

If you have any questions about changing your name, or run into any issues, organizations like Mermaids should be able to give you advice and support.

Changing your gender

Once you have changed your pronouns and your name, you may want to change the gender on your official documents.

Unfortunately, on many documents there is only the option to have your gender listed as 'male' or 'female'. If you don't identify as either, there may not be the option to have this listed as you might want. However, it's always worth asking; you can still follow the advice in this section, but prepare yourself for the fact that it may not end with your gender being correctly reflected in your records.

As with making sure your name is changed on your documents, the first thing to do is to sit down, by yourself or with someone you trust, and draw up a list of all the places you'll need to officially contact to change your gender and how best you can get in touch with them. You can then tick them off as you go!

Here are some that you might want to think about:

- Passport
- Driving licence (or provisional driving licence)
- School records
- Medical records
- Bank accounts.

Some of these places might require you to call them. If you have problems with phone calls, get a trusted person to make the call while you sit next to them. They might ask you to confirm that you are happy for this trusted person to speak for you, so you may have to answer some questions. Let them know you are autistic and you struggle with making calls, and answer their questions as best as you can. If you are non-verbal, you and your trusted person will need to make arrangements with the organization about what to do.

For your passport, you will have to apply for a new passport in order to change your gender marker. As this will cost around £75, it makes sense for you to change your name and gender marker on your passport at the same time. You can make these changes online: www.gov.uk/changing-passport-information. You can change your photo when you do this, if you've altered your appearance. There is currently no option to choose anything other than 'male' or 'female', although campaigners are working to try to change this.

Note: unlike changing your name, to change your gender marker on your passport you will have to provide either a Gender Recognition Certificate or a letter from your doctor or gender specialist confirming that your change of gender is 'permanent'. Gendered Intelligence has a template letter for your doctor to use here: http://genderedintelligence. co.uk/projects/kip/transitioning/docs/passport/doctorsletter.

For your driving licence, you will have to apply for a new licence, sending in your old licence and a letter requesting your gender marker be changed. You can change your photo when you do this, if you've altered your appearance slightly. Find out more here: www.gov.uk/change-name-driving-licence. Currently, only 'male' and 'female' are available as options.

The process of changing your gender marker on your medical records may depend on what GP surgery you go to. However, the guidelines state that doctor's surgeries *should* comply with requests to change your gender on your medical records. The best thing to do is to make an appointment to speak to the practice manager, and take with you any documents you have from your doctors at the gender identity clinic.

Some practices may ask for a Gender Recognition Certificate before agreeing to change your medical records – we'll look at that in the next section.

Once you have changed your gender marker on your medical records, please bear in mind that you may no longer be invited to routine screenings and tests that you may need for your health. For example, if you have a vagina you will still need to have smear tests, but the system won't automatically pick up that you need to be sent a reminder. You may need to keep track of what tests you have had in order to ensure you are getting what you need. You can find out more about the tests that may be impacted and what to do here: https://www.gov.uk/government/publications/nhs-population-screening-information-for-transgender-people/nhs-population-screening-information-for-trans-people.

Gendered Intelligence has lots of information on changing

your gender on documents here: http://genderedintelligence. co.uk/projects/kip/transitioning/docs.

If you have any questions about changing your gender, or run into any issues, organizations like Mermaids should be able to give you advice and support.

Gender Recognition Certificate
Changing your name and gender on your official documents does not mean that your gender is changed in the eyes of the law. The gender on your birth certificate will still be the gender that you were assigned at birth. However, you can change this by applying for a Gender Recognition Certificate.

You will have to submit an application to a Gender Recognition Panel, providing evidence that:

- you are over the age of 18
- you have lived as your 'acquired' gender (this is the words they use, even if it's not the words that trans people and others in the LGBTQIA+ community would use) for at least two years, and you intend to live as that gender for the rest of your life
- you have, or had, a diagnosis of gender dysphoria – you will need to provide two medical reports, one from your doctor and one from your gender specialist.

Although you don't have to have had any gender confirmation surgery (which we will look at briefly a bit further on) in order to get a Gender Recognition Certificate, they will probably ask why you haven't had any and whether you are planning to have it. If you don't want to have any surgery, you will probably be asked why you don't want it.

The fact that you are autistic shouldn't have an impact,

but it may be something that the panel wants to talk about. There are some people who believe that autistic people are less able to 'know' what they want, or aren't able to make such a big decision as to legally change their gender.

There are some really good resources that you might want to include in your application listed here: www.autism.org. uk/about/what-is/gender.aspx.

The process of getting a Gender Recognition Certificate is not perfect and may be frustrating.

There has been work by trans and non-binary campaigners and organizations to reform the Gender Recognition Act (which introduced Gender Recognition Certificates and allowed trans people to legally change their gender), and a consultation was held by the UK government in 2018. However, any changes seem to have been paused, which is disappointing.

Campaigners asked that Gender Recognition Certificates be changed to include non-binary people and other people who don't identify as male or female. They also asked for the process of getting a Gender Recognition Certificate to be easier, as trying to 'prove' you have lived as your gender to a panel of strangers can be difficult and unpleasant. Many countries allow people to legally change their gender through 'self-determination' – this basically means that if you say you are a certain gender, you do not have to prove it to a panel in order to be legally recognized as that gender.

Campaigners and organizations are still fighting for these changes, if you want to get involved:

- www.stonewall.org.uk/gender-recognition-act
- www.transactual.org.uk/the-gender-recognition-act

- https://mermaidsuk.org.uk/mermaids-manifesto-for-gra-reform.

If you want to apply for a Gender Recognition Certificate, you can get support from these organizations as well.

Looking how you want to look

As well as changing your name, pronouns and legal gender, it's likely that expressing your gender through your appearance will also be an important part of transitioning.

This may mean finding clothes that fit how you want to express your gender. For example, if you are a trans woman, wearing more traditionally 'feminine' clothes may be incredibly important for you. If you identify as neither a man nor a woman, you might prefer more 'androgynous' (meaning neither traditionally masculine nor feminine) clothes. If you are gender fluid, the clothes you wear might shift and change depending on how you feel.

It's important to remember that your gender expression does not impact your gender identity. You can be a trans man and still prefer to express yourself in a traditionally 'feminine' way – you are still a man, however you prefer to dress.

As autistic people, finding clothes that we're comfortable in can be difficult for us. We may find a certain type or brand of clothing that is comfortable for us, but doesn't quite 'fit' the traditional expression of our gender. Likewise, the clothes that we may be 'expected' to wear as a certain gender may be a complete sensory nightmare.

This is why it's so important to remember that your clothes do not define your gender.

For some people, wearing clothes traditionally associated

with their assigned gender at birth may trigger their dysphoria. In that case, you may need to dress a certain way in order to avoid distress, even if you are physically uncomfortable in those clothes. In other cases, you may be able to find clothes that you are comfortable in and change them slightly to fit how you want or need to express your gender (changing colour, adding details etc.).

Traditionally feminine looks	Traditionally masculine looks	Looks that can be androgynous
• Dresses • Skirts • Blouses (shirts that are shaped to the traditionally feminine body) • Shaped t-shirts • Skinny (or shaped) jeans • Leggings or tights • Clothes in colours like pink, red, purple and yellow • Clothes with flowery or soft designs • High heels • Platform shoes • Flats (found in the 'women's' department of shoe shops) • Longer hair • Jewellery • Make-up • Handbags	• Shirts • T-shirts (baggy t-shirts can be best for looking traditionally masculine) • Hoodies • Baggy jeans • Jogging bottoms • Sports kits • Clothes in colours like blue, green, brown and black • Clothes with harsher or graphic designs • Trainers • Boots • Dress shoes • Shorter hair • Backpacks • Small jewellery like a gold or silver chain or a single earring	In our society, most traditionally masculine clothes are also considered 'androgynous' in a way that traditionally feminine clothes aren't. However, there is no traditional way to be androgynous, so you might want to mix up things from both columns.

Remember: these things don't define your gender identity. They are only ways that you can choose how to express your gender. If you are a man, but you find you prefer traditionally feminine looks, that doesn't stop you from being a man.

You might hear people talking about 'passing'. This means when trans people 'pass' as their gender rather than their assigned gender – for example, if a trans man 'passes', it means people automatically assume he is a man, and do not question his gender.

For some trans people, passing is incredibly important. You might find that passing as your true gender helps with your dysphoria.

However, not every trans person is able to 'pass' as their gender as easily as others. This may lead to people misgendering you, which might be upsetting or cause you pain. It's important to remember that other people's opinions do not impact on who you are.

As well as adapting how you dress, there are other things you can do to express your gender in a way that fits your gender identity, and to help towards 'passing' as best you can, if that helps you.

Binding
This is when you wrap something around your chest in order to flatten it (you are less likely to be seen as a 'woman' if you don't have visible breasts). You should look at investing in a proper binder, as binding incorrectly could cause serious harm to your back, your ribs and your breathing. Your physical wellbeing is important. Some people use a special kind of tape to bind, which is designed to release moisture and breathe.

Popular binder brands include gc2b and Underworks. Popular binding tape brands include Transtape.

Remember that you can look around and get opinions from other people before deciding what works for you.

Important: binding for long periods of time can damage your health. As well as making sure you have the right kind of binder, consider using baggy tops some days instead of binding, to make your chest less pronounced and make you look more traditionally masculine. If binding causes a rash, or pain, do speak to a doctor.

Packing

This is when you put something in your underwear or trouser to give the impression that you have a penis. You can do this by rolling up a sock and popping it in your underwear, or you can get something that is designed to look like a penis.

There are lots of different types of packers. Some are more expensive than others. As you will be wearing one in your underwear, it's important to find one that looks *and* feels comfortable for you. You might prefer a soft packer that has a realistic feel, or you might prefer one that is more solid but creates a more realistic shape in your underwear.

Some packers can also be used to pee through and to use when having sex with your partner.

There are a lot of expensive packers around, but start off trying something a bit cheaper, and see how you feel. For some people, packers either don't do anything to help with dysphoria, or they can occasionally make dysphoria worse (because you can feel that it's not actually attached to your body), so see if it works for you before spending a lot of money.

Padding

This is when you add padding in your clothes to make your

chest look bigger and/or your hips look wider. You can buy specially made underwear for this, or you can add soft padding (e.g. rolled up fabric) that suits your sensory needs to your existing clothes. If you buy a padded bra, remember to make sure that the bra is the right size for your body and isn't too tight around your back or over your shoulders.

Try out some cheaper options before investing in something expensive, to make sure you are comfortable with it, as they will be against your skin. Find a material that works for you. Managing your dysphoria is important, but it's also important to think about your sensory needs to make sure you don't add unnecessary distress.

Remember: however you express your gender, whatever clothes you wear, whatever pronouns you use, and whatever name you go by, you are the gender that you say you are. Nobody gets to tell you that you aren't. It's always a good idea to try things out – names, pronouns, gender expression – if you're not 100 per cent sure about your gender identity, to see what fits you best. If you realize, later on down the line, that you aren't the gender you previously thought you were, that's perfectly fine and you can explore other options. This is your gender, your life, and there is no wrong way to do it.

Medical transition

If you transition medically, it means that you either take medication or have surgery to alter your body in some way to fit your gender identity.

There is no set route for people to medically transition. It may all depend on what exactly *you* have dysphoria about, and which areas of your body cause you the most distress. If you close your eyes and imagine how you want your body to be, this might help you to work out whether a medical transition is what you need, and what type of treatments would be best for you.

Most treatments and surgeries are only available to people over the age of 18, so we won't be going into them in detail here. However, we will have a brief look at them so you can start thinking about what might work best for you when you're older.

There are some medical treatments that *are* available for people under the age of 18, and we'll look at these first.

Puberty blockers

Puberty blockers (also known as hormone blockers) are medication designed to stop or slow down puberty.

They have been used for various reasons over the decades, particularly for people suffering from precocious puberty (where puberty occurs when the person is very young, and it can be debilitating and distressing). They can also be taken by young trans people to delay puberty, and to stop some of the changes to your body that might be distressing for you (for example: growing breasts, widening hips, facial hair, voice dropping, penis growth etc.).

Puberty blockers can be helpful, even if you aren't 100% sure of your gender identity. It can give you time to figure out who you are without going through the potential distress of permanent changes to your body.

However, they aren't always easy to get hold of. You will need to be in touch with a specialist who can refer you for hormone blocker treatments. If you are already in touch with a Gender Identity Clinic, please speak to them about the possibility of hormone blockers.

If you don't have supportive or understanding parents, or you don't have a trusted person to help you ask for puberty blockers, you can get in touch with an organization like Mermaids, which specializes in helping young trans people.

You may find people using your autism to question your decision to take puberty blockers. Often this stems from a misunderstanding of autism. See 'Information on autism' under the 'More information' section at the end of this chapter for some links and resources to help them understand autism, and hopefully dispel any myths about autistic trans people.

If you can't get access to puberty blockers, and you feel you are going through the 'wrong' puberty, please reach out to an organization like Mermaids or Gendered Intelligence. They can help support you through the distress that you might be feeling. As trans activists and writers Owl and Fox Fisher said in their *Trans Teen Survival Guide* (p.85):

> Most importantly, you have to remember that you will get through it. No matter how hopeless it might seem, no matter how hard it might be, there is always a light at the end of the tunnel. There are always options and there are always ways. There is a community out there that can support you, so seek the support you deserve.

Once you are old enough (usually around 16) you can consider whether or not you would like to start hormone therapy.

In 2020, a High Court decision potentially made it more difficult for people under the age of 16 to access puberty blockers. There is an appeal ongoing, and many activists and advocates are fighting against the decision. This is an ever-changing situation and it's likely that the information in this book may be out of date by the time it's published. Do not despair. Just keep an eye on what is happening, continue to ask for puberty blockers if you need them, and reach out to trans people and organisations for support.

Hormone therapy

This is when you take hormones that are different from the ones you produce naturally. You might hear it called hormone replacement therapy (HRT). You might also hear people talking about taking 'cross-hormones', which means that they are taking hormones that are different from the ones their body produces naturally.

Hormone therapy will cause changes to your body in line with your true gender identity. However, the types of changes you experience will depend on how far through puberty you have gone – for example, if you have completed puberty, the effects won't be as strong as for someone who takes hormone blockers from a young age and doesn't experience full puberty.

If you are taking cross-hormones, it's likely you will also be prescribed blockers (a different kind to puberty blockers) to stop your body producing the hormones it naturally produces.

Remember: even if there is a long wait for hormone therapy, do not look for alternatives online. There are a lot of people out there who might take advantage of your desperation. I know that it's distressing having to wait, but anything other than officially prescribed hormone therapy could cause you real harm. You deserve to be safe and well.

There are two different types of hormone therapy you can take, depending on your gender.

Testosterone (or T)

This is the hormone you will most likely be prescribed if you are a trans man or trans-masculine. Some of the effects of taking T include your voice dropping, more hair growing on your face and body, changes in how your fat is distributed on your body and it becoming easier to build up your muscles.

As an autistic person, some of these changes may be incredibly uncomfortable while they are happening. For example, you may struggle with the feeling of extra hair on your body, often growing in places where you're not used to it. Have a play around with what is comfortable for you – remember, if you need to shave some of this extra hair to be comfortable, it doesn't make you any less of a man or any less masculine.

If you have a clitoris, you may find that taking T makes it grow bigger (sometimes to the point where it will look like a micro-penis). As there are a *lot* of nerve endings in this area, this is likely to be very sensitive and take a while to get used to. Make sure you play around with different types of underwear, and different materials, to find something that suits your sensory needs.

If you are struggling with how this feels and it's causing you some distress, reach out to a service like Mermaids which may be able to offer you support or direct you to where you can speak to other people on T to talk about your experiences.

You can take T in two different ways: you can have injections, usually every few weeks or couple of months (depending on your individual situation) or you can rub gel into your body every day. The effects of the injection tend to happen faster.

When discussing taking T, make sure you (or your trusted person) talk with the specialist about your specific sensory needs – if you struggle to take injections, then the gel may be best, whereas if you struggle with the thought of gel on your body, the injection may be best. This may be a bigger issue that needs considering because you are autistic, and it's important to let the specialist know this.

Oestrogen (or O)

This is the hormone you will most likely be prescribed if you are a trans woman or trans-feminine. Some of the effects of taking O include softer skin, changes in the distribution of fat in your body (there will probably be more of it in your breasts, hips and bottom) and the texture of the hair on your body, and breast growth.

As an autistic person, some of these changes may be incredibly uncomfortable while they are happening. As your breasts grow, they are likely to become very sensitive and might even be sore, and you'll have to look at finding a bra that is comfortable. It's important to make sure you have the right size bra, and to play around with what types of bra are comfortable for you – some clothes shops, especially shops specifically selling bras, can help you measure your bra size in store. It's a good idea to get in touch beforehand to see if they offer this service, and to let them know that you are autistic and what your specific sensory issues are.

Unlike T, O doesn't affect beard growth and doesn't affect your voice. If these things are distressing for you, or trigger your dysphoria, there are other things you can do. For your facial hair, this might mean daily shaving or more permanent treatments such as laser treatment. For your voice, this might mean having voice training lessons or looking at vocal cord surgeries later down the line.

As O isn't as strong as T, it's likely you will have to take blockers to stop the T your body naturally produces. You may also take progesterone, a hormone that helps you to grow breasts, and can also help with fat distribution throughout your body. It's a good idea to talk about these options with your specialist.

You can take O in three different ways: pills that you take regularly, patches on your skin that have to be changed every few months, and injections which can last for a few weeks (although these aren't available everywhere).

When discussing taking O, make sure you (or your trusted person) talk with the specialist about your specific sensory needs – if you struggle with patches on your skin, then the pills may be best, whereas if you struggle with swallowing pills, the patches may be best. This may be a bigger issue that needs considering because you are autistic, and it's important to let the specialist know this.

Remember: taking cross-hormones for a long period of time can affect your fertility. This might not be something that you're thinking about right now, but it might be something that you care about in the future. Talk with your doctor or specialist about this, particularly the option of freezing and storing your eggs or sperm.

Surgeries

While for many trans people the effects of hormone therapy are enough to fight off dysphoria, as you become an adult, you might decide that you want to have surgery to make bigger changes to your body. This is a very brief overview of surgeries that are available. You do not have to have all of the surgeries, or even *any* of the surgeries, if you don't want them – you are still your true gender, with or without them. It's purely your choice.

For trans men and trans-masculine people

- *Top surgery* (breast removal or subcutaneous mastectomy) – surgery to remove your breasts and flatten your chest.
- *Hysterectomy* – surgery to remove all or part of your uterus or womb (your reproductive system). This will stop your monthly periods.
- *Metoidioplasty* – surgery that takes an enlarged clitoris (which has grown as a result of taking T, which we talked about earlier) and makes it look more like a penis by changing the surrounding tissue and adding prosthetic testicles (if you want).
- *Phalloplasty* – surgery that builds a whole penis using donor skin and tissue from another part of your body (often the arm).

For trans women and trans-feminine people

- *Breast augmentation* – surgery to enlarge your breasts using implants.
- *Orchiectomy* – surgery to remove one or both testicles (if you have your testicles removed, you will no longer have to take hormone blockers, as most testosterone in the body is produced in the testicles).
- *Vaginoplasty (different types of vaginoplasty)* – surgery to remove the penis and testicles and create a new vagina

(functional, meaning it has depth). There are different types of this surgery, and your doctor will discuss which is best for you.

- *Vulvoplasty (Zero Depth Vaginoplasty)* – surgery to remove the penis and testicles and create a vulva (so on the outside it looks like you have a vagina, but it doesn't actually go inside the body).
- *Facial/Body feminization surgery* – surgery that can be performed on your face and body to make you appear more traditionally feminine (e.g., softening the jaw line, or moving fat around in your body to give you wider hips).

Remember: all surgeries carry risk, and recovering from surgery can be long and painful. If you are thinking about surgery, reach out to other trans people, particularly autistic trans people, who have had the surgery so you know what to expect. If you decide not to pursue any surgery, you are not 'failing' at being your true gender. Some trans people do not pursue surgery at all – you can have breasts and a vagina and be a man, you can have a penis and small breasts and be a woman, and you can have any of these and be non-binary.

Stopping or starting your transition

Your transition is down to you, and you can start or stop whenever you want. These are big decisions for you to make, and you deserve to have the time and space to think about them. Although it's important to discuss things with specialists, and with other trusted people in your life, it's also important to do what is best for you.

You might begin to transition, either socially or medically, and find that, actually, this isn't right for you. This is okay.

Some people call this 'detransitioning' – where someone begins to transition, and then decides that actually they identify with the gender they were assigned at birth. Wherever you are in your transition, you are allowed to step back and look at whether what you are doing is right for you.

If you do decide to stop transitioning, or think you may want to detransition, there is support for you within the trans community. Don't be afraid to reach out and discuss your feelings. There is an organization that has been set up for destransitioners called the Detransitioners Advocacy Network but its work has been called into serious question. There are also a lot of dubious resources if you google 'detransitioning'. It's best to reach out to the trans community and to trans organizations for support and advice on this issue.

If you do stop your transition, or realize that you are cis, this does not make you a traitor to the community. You have not let anyone down. The trans people around you and in the community want you to figure out who you are and be happy more than anything else.

There is no right or wrong way to transition. Whatever you do, make sure you are safe, and make sure you are doing what makes you happy.

More information

Books

Trans Teen Survival Guide by Owl and Fox Fisher

LGBTQ: The Survival Guide for Lesbian, Gay, Bisexual, Transgender, and Questioning Teens by Kelly Huegel Madrone

The Pride Guide: A Guide to Sexual and Social Health for LGBTQ Youth by Jo Langford

Transgender 101: A Simple Guide to a Complex Issue by Nicholas M. Teich

Links

Mermaids: https://mermaidsuk.org.uk/young-people/resources-for-young-people

Gendered Intelligence: http://genderedintelligence.co.uk/project/kip/genderex

Gendered Intelligence: http://genderedintelligence.co.uk/projects/kip/transitioning

NHS: www.nhs.uk/conditions/gender-dysphoria/treatment

YouTube videos

FTM Outro || Transition Start to Finish by Jammidodger: http://bit.do/FTM-Outro

Trans Guys Comparing Transitions ft. Noah Finnce by Jammidodger: http://bit.do/Trans-Guys-Comparing-Transitions
In the first video, Jamie looks back from the beginning of his transition to the present, including all the changes that took place along the way. In the second video, Jamie and Noah compare their experiences with transitioning. Jamie has lots of videos on his channel detailing his experiences with hormones and various surgeries.

I'm Transgender Playlist by Mathilda Hogberg: http://bit.do/Im-Transgender
In this playlist, there are a lot of videos where Mathilda talks about her experiences with transitioning, what it's like to be on hormones, surgeries and coming out to people as trans after transitioning.

The Sex Education You Never Had *PRIDE EDITION* by Ellbat: http://
bit.do/Sex-Education-You-Never-Had
In this hour-long video, Ellbat (with an appearance by Fox Fisher)
answers lots of questions about all things LGBTQIA+, including
common questions around transitioning, binding, pronouns and
attending gender identity clinics. You can find the questions you
need answering, and what time they appear in the video, in the
description box for easy access to information.

*There are lots of other YouTube videos about transitioning, but be
aware: if you search 'transitioning', there are a lot of videos about
detransitioning, and this may give you the impression that detransitioning is common. While the experiences of detransitioners are real
and valid, they are not the experiences of the majority of people who
transition. The number of videos you find does not necessarily equal
the percentage of trans people who have those experiences.*

Information on autism

The National Autistic Society has a comprehensive webpage on what
autism is, what autistic people might experience, and what autism isn't
(www.autism.org.uk/about/what-is.aspx)

Wenn Lawson, a trans autistic man and researcher of 20 years, has several
books published, and also gave an interview about his experiences of gender
and autism on Network Autism (https://network.autism.org.uk/knowledge/
insight-opinion/interview-dr-wenn-lawson-autism-and-gender-dysphoria)

Joe Butler, an SEN and disability consultant, has written about supporting
trans or gender questioning autistic pupils in a school environment, and
it may be useful to share this with any gender professionals who don't
understand (https://network.autism.org.uk/knowledge/insight-opinion/
supporting-trans-and-gender-questioning-autistic-pupils)

Jay Avery, a non-binary autistic writer and activist, wrote a piece for the
Huffington Post about why being autistic doesn't mean you aren't trans
(including links to studies and information that might be helpful) (www.
huffingtonpost.co.uk/jay-avery/trans-autism_b_14418218.html)

CHAPTER 6

LGBTQIA+ Relationships and Friendships

Relationships of all kinds are incredibly important, particularly in a community like the LGBTQIA+ community.

There is something very special about forming relationships with people who understand and accept you for who you are. You may hear the phrase 'chosen family' used by LGBTQIA+ people to describe these relationships – people they have met, formed bonds with, and chosen to have as their family separately to their 'real' family.

These types of relationships are especially important to LGBTQIA+ people. There is a long history of us being isolated from our 'official' family and friends due to our sexuality and gender, and so the idea of 'found' or 'chosen' family has a strong emotional meaning in the community. There are still people today whose family react badly to them coming out (as we discussed in the chapter on coming out), so relationships with other people in the LGBTQIA+ community are just as important as they ever were.

Even if your family is accepting and loving, relationships within the community can still be very important. They certainly have been for me.

There is more than one kind of relationship you can have. This includes friendships, queerplatonic relationships, romantic relationships, sexual relationships, and others. Romantic or sexual relationships might include one partner (monogamy) or several partners (polygamy). One type of relationship is not more important or more valid than another. All relationships are important.

All types of relationships can be wonderful. But all types of relationships can also be abusive. It's important to talk about all of them and how to stay safe.

We'll be looking at issues around sex, consent and sexual abuse in the next chapter. But in this chapter, we're going to focus on the emotional bit of relationships – types of relationships, making sure your relationships are healthy, figuring out if a relationship has become toxic or abusive, and ending unhealthy relationships.

Types of relationships

As we said, there are lots of different types of relationships. We'll have a look at some of them here.

Friendships

A friendship is described as 'a bond of mutual affection between people'. Your friends are people you will have a strong emotional connection with.

Some friendships are formed when you are in the same

place as a person for a long time (e.g. at school or at work). Lots of friendships are formed by connecting over a similar interest. This is especially common for autistic people, who are more likely to have strong interests and form strong emotional connections with other people around those interests.

Being part of the LGBTQIA+ community could, in itself, be considered a shared interest, and friends can form from it. In the same way, being specifically autistic in the LGBTQIA+ community can be a shared interest, and friends can come from that. If the basis of your friendship is just 'we're both queer' or 'we're both autistic', then that is as valid as any other friendship.

Friends in the LGBTQIA+ community can be very intense, because not everyone outside the community is always friendly to us. Other LGBTQIA+ people understand what it's like to be LGBTQIA+.

Autistic people can also form very intense friendships, with other autistic people or non-autistic people. We can form incredibly powerful bonds and friendships, sometimes even obsessive. We are likely to be very open about things in our lives, and be quicker to tell people personal things about ourselves than non-autistic people. This can help form firm friendships, but it also means we can be taken advantage of.

We'll look at toxic or abusive relationships, including friendships, later on in the chapter.

Whether you find friends in your area, out in the LGBTQIA+ community (we'll be discussing going out and about in the community in a later chapter), or even online, they will likely be an important part of your life.

Romantic relationships
A romantic relationship is a close emotional bond between

people that is different from a friendship, in that it may be more physically or emotionally intimate. If you are in a romantic relationship with someone, this might be the person you refer to as your girlfriend, boyfriend, theyfriend, partner, significant other, husband, wife, spouse or other term associated with being romantically connected to someone.

People in romantic relationships are said to be 'in love' with each other. This is a slightly different feeling than loving someone – you can love a friend, a family member, a pet, a fictional character, but it's not the same as being 'in love' romantically. The feelings can be tricky to separate, and it can be important to discuss what you're feeling with someone you trust (either talking about it out loud, or through an online chat, or any other ways of communication that work for you).

Sometimes the line between friendship and romance may be slightly blurred. This is certainly something that I have struggled with, particularly in friendships that get very intense (I have very intense friendships due to my autistic nature). Someone may be your friend, and you may have romantic feelings towards them, but this does not mean you are in a romantic relationship. Romantic relationships are partnerships – the romantic and emotional feelings are mutual, and have usually been discussed and agreed on.

We'll look at what to do if you find yourself falling in love with, or having romantic feelings for, someone you class as a 'friend' later on in this chapter.

Many romantic relationships are also sexual relationships, but they don't have to be. Having sex or being physically intimate with someone is seen as a core part of a romantic relationship (particularly in books and films), but you can have a healthy romantic relationship without these things. A romantic relationship may include sex, but it's about feelings (sex is often a part of those feelings, but it doesn't have to be).

Queerplatonic relationships

A queerplatonic relationship is described as 'an umbrella term for any relationship that bends the rules for telling apart romantic relationships from non-romantic relationships'. It came from the asexual community, and has recently started to be used more and more.

Some people don't like this term, but I really do like it. It's a term that I've found very useful in defining relationships that aren't quite romantic in the traditional way, but are also more committed and connected than what would traditionally be called a 'friendship'.

As an autistic person, it's really important for me to find the right words to describe things. Finding a word that *sort of* fits doesn't work for me. So having a word like 'queerplatonic' is really useful for me.

Traditionally, there are strict boundaries between things that friends do, and things that romantic partners do. For example, romantic relationships may be seen as more physically affectionate, or emotionally close, than friendships. Things like moving in together, getting married or having children are seen as things that happen in romantic relationships, and not friendships.

If your relationship with someone blurs these traditional lines (e.g. people in queerplatonic relationships may not see themselves as romantic partners, but may live together, get married or raise children), then you may want to say that this is a queerplatonic relationship. If you have a relationship with someone which feels like more than a friendship, but calling it a romantic relationship doesn't feel right, then you may want to say this is a queerplatonic relationship.

There isn't a solid definition of a queerplatonic relationship, so it's up to you whether you describe your relationship in this way. Make sure that you discuss it with your potential partner or partners before you begin using the term. Once there is an agreement between you, you can play around with the term, explore it, and see if it works for your relationship.

Sexual relationships

Although we're going to be looking at sex in the next chapter, it's a good idea to very quickly go over sexual relationships.

If you have a sexual relationship with someone, it means that sex or sexual contact (taking part in any sort of sex act together) is a part of your relationship.

Sexual relationships can also be romantic relationships or friendships. As we said a little bit earlier, many romantic relationships are also sexual relationships. Sex may be an important part of romance for you.

Sexual relationships don't have to be romantic relationships. You might be in a sexual relationship that is also a friendship – you may have an emotional connection, and be sexually attracted to each other, but it might not go as far as wanting to be romantic partners. This is sometimes called a 'friends with benefits' relationship. However, if you are in a relationship like this, and either you or your partner wants it to become a romantic relationship but the other partner doesn't, it's a good idea to step away from the sexual element of the relationship.

This is to avoid feelings getting hurt and the relationship becoming unequal.

As with any relationship, all sexual relationships have the

possibility to be toxic or abusive. We'll be looking at consent and sexual abuse in the next chapter. However, in this chapter we will be looking at how to spot if a relationship is becoming toxic and abusive – it's important to bear those things in mind for sexual relationships as well.

Monogamy and polyamory

Sometimes, relationships can be specifically between two people. Other times, relationships can be between more than two people.

Friendship groups are often made up of more than two people. You will likely have individual relationships with each of those friends, but you will then have a group relationship dynamic when you're all together.

When people think about a romantic relationship, they often think of it being between two people. Many romantic relationships are exclusive between two people, but other romantic relationships have more than one person involved.

We're going to have a very quick look at these two things: monogamy and polyamory.

Monogamy
This is when you have a romantic and/or sexual relationship with one person at one time.

It means that if you are in a romantic relationship with someone, you are not having romantic relationships with anyone else.

If that romantic relationship is sexual, it means that you are not having sexual relationships or contact with anyone else.

Having a monogamous relationship is a decision that

you and your partner make together. If one person in the relationship is monogamous, but the other person is not (is still having romantic and/or sexual relationships with other people), then that is not a healthy relationship. Monogamy is something that you have to talk about and agree on as a couple.

If one partner wants to be monogamous, and one partner doesn't, then you need to have a serious conversation about whether this relationship is right for you.

Polyamory

This is when you have romantic and/or sexual relationships with more than one person at one time.

This can take several different forms.

You might be in a romantic and/or sexual relationship with someone, and agree that you can have other romantic and/or sexual relationships with other people outside that relationship (this often gets called an 'open' relationship).

You might be in a romantic and/or sexual relationship with more than one person, and the people you are in those relationships with may be friends or see themselves as family.

You might be in a romantic and/or sexual relationship with more than one person, and the people you are in those relationships with may also be in romantic and/or sexual relationships with each other.

Having a polyamorous relationship is a decision that you and you partner make together. Not everyone is comfortable with polyamory, just as not everyone is comfortable with monogamy. Polyamory, and how those relationships work, is something that you have to talk about and agree on as a couple or as a group of partners.

If you have not agreed to be polyamorous, and you and

your partner have other romantic and/or sexual relationships anyway, then that is cheating. This is not a healthy relationship.

If one partner wants to be monogamous, and the other partner doesn't, then you need to have a serious conversation about whether this relationship is right for you.

Remember: whatever type of relationship you prefer, it is totally valid and good. You do not have to do anything that you are uncomfortable with. If your partner (or partners) puts pressure on you to do one thing or another, or threatens to leave if you don't try something you don't want to try, then that is not a healthy relationship. We'll have more information on recognizing and getting out of toxic or abusive relationships later on in the chapter.

Tips for healthy relationships

What works best for your relationships might not be exactly the same as what works for someone else's relationships, but there are some basic things that healthy relationships rely on. These things apply to friendships as well as romantic, sexual or queerplatonic relationships.

Respect
You must respect the other person/people in the relationship. They must also respect you. This includes respecting people's pronouns, how they identify (gender or sexuality), what they like, what they don't like, when they say 'no', and their right to privacy. Respecting someone also means not making fun of them in a nasty way, not calling them names, not talking down to them or making them feel bad about things they can't change.

Boundaries

It's important to set boundaries in a relationship. For example, if your partner does something you don't like, such as talking about a certain thing or touching you a particular way, it's important to say you don't like it and you would like it to stop. In a healthy relationship, this would be respected. Respecting boundaries also includes things like not checking the other person's phone or social media without their permission, not having to know where the other person is at all times, and allowing the other person to have a life and friendships outside your particular relationship.

Fairness/Equality

You should be equal partners in the relationship. However, this doesn't mean that everything in the relationship must be split down the middle. Some people may require more support than others (e.g. if you are autistic and the other person is not, there may be some things that you can't do and that you might need more support with), and this doesn't make a relationship unfair. It does not make you a burden. However, it's important to talk about what you can both do, and work out how to make sure you're both doing what you can. You must all care about and love each other equally.

Communication

Whether the relationship is between you and another autistic person, or you and a non-autistic person, you'll have to figure out what works best for you. You may find it comfortable to sit down and talk about things. It might make sense to put a regular time to chat in the schedule – make it a part of your routine. My family does this by having a meeting every night. We chat about what's happening the next day, and about how we are feeling, and whether we want to talk about anything that's happened that day.

However, if having these conversations in person is difficult for you, there are lots of other ways to communicate and keep your relationship healthy. You might prefer to use text or chat features on your phone. Or you might like to write things down as you think them, and share them with the other person. You might even have some sort of word or signal to let the other person know that you are struggling and need some support (even if you can't put it into words).

Trust/Honesty

This is really important. You must be able to trust the other person, and you must earn and keep their trust as well. This means not lying to them about things (like where you have been, how you're feeling etc.), and about being as honest as you possibly can about everything. There may be some small secrets that you have, or some feelings that you only share with certain people like best friends, and it is okay to not be a completely open book to everyone. You have to work out what levels of honesty work for each relationship. For example, it's not dishonest to lie to someone by not telling them what you're getting them for their birthday!

As autistic people, we are more likely to disclose a lot about ourselves very quickly. Any person who learns intimate things about you must earn your trust by not repeating those things to anyone else, or using those things against you. People may not always know if something you've told them is private or not, so make sure you tell them whether they need to keep it to themselves. If your partner tells you something, make sure you ask them whether it's private or something you can share.

Remember: there may be other things that are important to you in a relationship, or other things that you need to make your relationships healthy. You might make mistakes as you try to figure it out. We have all made mistakes in relationships. Keep a note of what works for you, if you think that will help.

What if I get a crush on my friend?

Having romantic or sexual feelings for your friends is something that a lot of people, not just LGBTQIA+ people, go through. It can be very complicated and difficult. I've gone through it several times, and sometimes there's no solution that won't hurt a little bit. But it's okay, and as much as it seems like the end of the world, you will get through it.

If you have feelings for a friend, or if you think you might have feelings for a friend but aren't sure, it's not a good idea to sit on it and let the feelings bubble. The longer it goes on, the more the feelings get stronger, and the more you might fantasize about things that aren't going to happen in real life. It's a good idea to communicate about it – with a trusted person, and then with the friend in question.

It might be as simple as writing them an email or a text or a letter that says: *I have these feelings for you, do you have these feelings for me?*

If they say 'yes', or say they want to try dating, then fantastic! But remember that it might not be what you imagined in your head. It still might not work.

If they say 'no', then this is something you will have to deal with. People do not owe you their romantic or sexual feelings, no matter how close you are or what you think you have done to deserve it. The same applies to you – you don't owe anyone your romantic or sexual feelings.

Raising your feelings might make your relationship awkward for a little while. You might find yourself feeling angry, resentful and upset that your friend doesn't return your feelings. This is normal, but you have to try to deal with it. It might help to speak to someone you trust about your feelings. If you're not comfortable with this, writing down your feelings might help (whether you share them with anyone is up to you, but it might be helpful).

It's going to hurt. There's not anything you can do to stop it hurting completely. But there are things you can do to distract yourself: focusing on your interests, taking up new hobbies and spending time with other people doing fun things can be a good way to help you get through it.

With any luck, your friendship with the person will be able to continue. But, if it doesn't, then it might be best for both of you.

Abusive relationships

As we've seen, relationships can be brilliant, complicated, wonderful, life-affirming and important.

However, all relationships can also be abusive. Whether we're talking about a friendship, a romantic relationship, a queerplatonic relationship, or any other kind of relationship you might have with another person, there is always the possibility that the relationship will become toxic and harmful.

Anyone of any gender and sexuality can be abusive. And anyone of any gender or sexuality can be abused. Abuse might be physical. But it can also come in the form of emotional abuse, coercive control (when someone controls every aspect of the other person's life) and sexual abuse.

As autistic and LGBTQIA+ people, we can be particularly

vulnerable to abuse. As a young, newly out bisexual woman at university, who was desperate to find relationships with people in the community, I was a prime target for a toxic relationship. On top of that, as a young autistic woman, I was filled with anxiety, struggling with socializing in the LGBTQIA+ community, and had real trouble reading people's intentions. I also had a tendency to form intense, almost obsessive relationships with people who showed me kindness or interest.

As a result of all this, I found myself in a very toxic and abusive friendship. I didn't realize that it was abusive until several years later. I never believed that friendships could be abusive. I believed only romantic relationships could be abusive. But that's what it was. And it had a lasting impact on me.

If I'd been able to recognize it earlier, I might have been able to get some help and walk away.

So we're going to have a look at what abusive relationships might look like. These red flags apply to all kinds of relationships, so please do take note. You deserve to be safe, happy and protected.

What does an abusive relationship look like?

Here are some questions to ask yourself about your relationships.

- Does the other person make you feel bad (by calling you names, making fun of you in a way you don't like, making you feel small, mocking your appearance)?
- Does the other person invade your privacy (by tracking your phone, logging into your social media, checking your messages without your permission)?

- Does the other person have a problem with you speaking to/going out with your friends and family (accusing you of spending too much time with them, trying to cause problems and fights in your other relationships, saying that you don't 'need' other people if you love them)?

- Does the other person constantly accuse you of doing something wrong (cheating, lying to them, hiding things from them)?

- Does the other person get angry with you for no reason (for being too loud, or too quiet, or not doing something exactly how they want it, or not making a decision quickly enough etc.)?

- Does the other person try to control everything you do (and are you afraid of not doing what they ask, and anxious that anything you do could make them angry)?

- Does the other person make fun of you because of your autism (calling you names, acting as if you can't make your own decisions, treating you like a child)?

- Does the other person refuse to respect your gender or sexuality (refusing to use the right pronouns, suggesting you're more likely to cheat because you're bisexual, accusing you of not being a 'proper' gay if you don't do certain things)?

- Does the other person try to control your money (taking money from you, not letting you decide what you buy with your own money, tracking what you spend, giving you 'pocket money')?

- Does the other person try to convince you of things that you know aren't true (this is often called 'gaslighting' – for example, my abusive friend drip fed me stories until I truly believed he was part of an underground MI6 agency)?

- Does the other person physically hurt you (hitting, kicking, spitting, grabbing you by the arm, pinching you, holding you too tightly – even if it has only happened once and they promised to never do it again)?
- Does the other person pressure you to have sex or do sexual things when you don't want to (by continuing to ask even after you've said 'no', by telling you that you 'owe' them sex, by having sex with you while you're asleep or very intoxicated, or by having sex with you despite you saying 'no')?

If you have answered 'yes' to any of these, then there is a chance that your relationship (friendship, romantic, sexual, queerplatonic, or other) might be toxic and unhealthy, and could very well be abusive. If they are physically hurting you or forcing you to have sex when you don't want to, this is *definitely* abusive.

As a young LGBTQIA+ person, you might find yourself forming relationships (friendships or romantic) with older people in the community. Often, older people who have been out for a while can be good friends who can guide you through all of the confusion that is growing up LGBTQIA+.

However, as they are older than you, there is a power dynamic that can be abused. If you are a teenager, and someone who is an adult is being inappropriate (talking to you a lot about sex, trying to control you, asking if you can date, sending you pictures), then the relationship is abusive.

They may tell you that you are mature for your age. They may tell you that love or friendship is about more than just a number. They may tell you that it's you against the world, and the rest of the world is wrong. These are abusive tactics to make you think that what is happening is okay. It isn't okay.

What can you do?

If you think your relationship might be abusive, the best thing you can do is leave. You deserve to be treated better than this. The longer you stay with an abusive person (partner or friend) the harder it can be to leave.

How you end the relationship depends on what your situation is. If the relationship is struggling because the other person is being rude or belittling you, sending them a message to tell them that you don't want to continue being their friend/partner anymore might be the best way. If you feel you can do it face to face, you can – but make sure you have someone with you if you need to.

As autistic people, we often struggle with these conversations. So sending a message (an email, a text, a chat message) might be easiest for you. This does not make you a bad person.

If you need to, you can also block these people on social media. You can also block phone numbers. If you suddenly stop responding to someone with no explanation, this is called 'ghosting'. This is generally considered a bad thing to do. So sending a message letting them know what you're doing before blocking them might be the best thing.

However, if you feel uncomfortable or threatened, your safety comes first. If you need to block them without letting them know what you're doing, then block them. If you aren't sure whether you should do this or not, you can get in touch with some of the organizations at the end of this chapter.

If you feel threatened, or are scared for your safety, then you might need to be more careful about how you get out of the relationship. If the person is physically abusive to you, then it may be harder to leave, especially if you live together. If you are going to leave, make sure you leave safely.

Here are some things to do:

- Create an emergency bag containing your important documents (such as birth certificate, ID documents), some keys, some clothes, any medication you need, a list of emergency contacts, and a phone charger (and a portable charging block, if you can get one). Only do this if you can do it safely, without the other person knowing.
- Put together a plan, making a note of the other person's routines and working out when is a good time to leave (when they aren't around). Make sure that the plan is safe – think about avoiding local taxi services, or using services with people who know the other person.
- Make sure you have a place to stay. This could be a friend, a family member, or it might be a domestic violence shelter. Not all domestic violence shelters accept all genders, so make sure you have been in contact with the shelter beforehand to check that they will accept you. You can also get advice from your local authority on housing, and whether they can organize housing where you can stay.
- Make sure that the other person can't track you through your electronics. Turn off the tracking on your phone, or turn your phone off and use someone else's until you can get a new one. Delete your search history, if you have been looking online for ways to find support.

Your safety is important. Getting advice from experienced people who can listen to your situation might be a key part of being able to stay safe. Have a look at and use the resources at the end of the chapter. These include ways to get in touch with such people if you can't make phone calls (as many of us can't).

Note: as well as being the victim of an abuser, there is always the chance that you might become the perpetrator of abuse or become a toxic person in a relationship. Make sure you read the checklist of things to look out for and think: am I doing any of this? If you think you might be, you can reach out to the same domestic violence charities and helplines and they can offer you advice or support. You can work to make your behaviour better, if you want to.

More information

Books

Gender Identity, Sexuality and Autism by Eva A. Mendes and Meredith R. Maroney

LGBTQ: The Survival Guide for Lesbian, Gay, Bisexual, Transgender, and Questioning Teens by Kelly Huegel Madrone

The Pride Guide: A Guide to Sexual and Social Health for LGBTQ Youth by Jo Langford

Doing It! Let's Talk About Sex by Hannah Witton (this is primarily about sex, but it has some good information about healthy relationships and spotting abuse)

YouTube videos

The Sex Education You Never Had *PRIDE EDITION* by Ellbat: http://bit.do/Sex-Education-You-Never-Had
In this hour-long video, Ellbat (with an appearance by Fox Fisher) answers lots of questions about all things LGBTQIA+, including

common questions around relationships and friendships if you're LGBTQIA+. You can find the questions you need answering, and what time they appear in the video, in the description box for easy access to information.

Resources if you're in an abusive relationship

Galop – An organization supporting LGBTQIA+ people who have experienced hate crime, domestic abuse or sexual violence

Website:
• www.galop.org.uk

Phone:
• 0800 999 5428 (Monday to Friday, 10am to 5pm; Wednesday and Thursday, 10am to 8pm)

Email:
• help@galop.org.uk

Online form:
• www.galop.org.uk/report

Webchat:
• In the bottom right-hand corner of the website, a blue box marked 'specialist web chat services'

The National Domestic Abuse Helpline – Run by Refuge, this is a support service for women and children who are experiencing or have experienced domestic violence

Website:
• www.nationaldahelpline.org.uk

Phone:
• 0808 2000 247 (open 24 hours a day)

Online Chat:
• www.nationaldahelpline.org.uk/Chat-to-us-online (Monday to Friday, 3pm to 6pm)

Send a message:
• www.nationaldahelpline.org.uk/Contact-us (if you need to be referred to a refuge, let them know and they can do this. However, if you are not a cis woman, double check that the support they offer is available to you)

Respect – An advice and support line for men who are experiencing or have experienced domestic violence

Website:

- https://mensadviceline.org.uk

Phone:

- 0808 8010327 (Monday to Friday, 9am to 8pm

Webchat:

- https://mensadviceline.org.uk/contact-us (Wednesday: 10am to 11am and 3pm to 4pm; Thursday: 10am to 11am and 3pm to 4pm; Friday: 10am to 11am and 3pm to 4pm)

Email:

- info@mensadviceline.org.uk

Childline – An advice and support service for children and young people in the UK provided by the NSPCC

Phone:

- 0800 1111 (free and open 24/7, although calls between midnight and 7.30am may be limited to 15 minutes)
- There are some Welsh-speaking counsellors. When calling, let them know that you would like to speak to someone in Welsh and a time will be arranged for you to do so

Online chat:

- www.childline.org.uk/get-support/1-2-1-counsellor-chat (click the box on the right-hand side to enter the waiting room. There is a traffic light system to indicate how busy the service is, and how long you might have to wait)

Art box:

- www.childline.org.uk/toolbox/art-box (this enables you to draw about how you are feeling. If you struggle to express yourself with words, or English isn't your first language, you can share what you draw with the counsellor you speak to in the online chat)
- You will need to create an account and sign in to save what you draw. You can do this by clicking on the box in the bottom right-hand corner next to the Art box

Message boards

- www.childline.org.uk/get-support/message-boards (you can chat with other young people who understand or may have gone through the same thing)

CHAPTER 7

Sex

There is more to being LGBTQIA+ than just who you are having sex with. But it's important to know about sex, sexual relationships and how to be safe.

The most important thing to remember is: you don't have to have sex or be in a relationship in order to prove you are LGBTQIA+. If you aren't ready to have sex, or be in a relationship, this doesn't make you any less LGBTQIA+ than someone who is. And if you are ready to have sex, or be in a relationship, or both, make sure you are safe and happy and comfortable when you do.

If you have had sex and relationships education in school, you will likely know a little bit about sex.

When I was a teenager, I was only told a few things about sex. Here is what I was told:

- Sex is when a man (as they would define a man) puts

his penis in a woman's (as they would define a woman) vagina.

- Foreplay is what happens before sex – it can involve you touching your body or your partner's body, or your partner touching your body, and it's about making you feel good before the act of sex (to make the act of sex feel better).
- Sex acts that don't involve putting a penis in a vagina can include using your tongue or your lips on your partner's genitals, or using your hands on your partner's genitals.
- Sex can lead to pregnancy if you don't use protection (condoms, the pill etc.).
- Sex can lead to sexually transmitted diseases if you don't use protection (condoms).

Although this does give some important points, it misses out an awful lot. It assumes that sex will be between a cisgender man and a cisgender woman. It also doesn't talk about consent, communicating during sex, or how to make sure that you and your partner are actually enjoying yourselves.

We'll have a quick look at how LGBTQIA+ people may have sex, how to stay safe, and how, as autistic people, we can make sure that sex is a good experience. But, first of all, we need to talk about something that is very important: consent.

Consent

Consent is one of the most important aspects of sex. Sex without consent isn't sex: it's rape. And it's important to understand it: what consent is, how to give it, and how to make sure that your partner is also consenting to everything you do.

If you are younger than 16, you are not legally able to consent to sex. If someone has sex with you, and you are younger than 16, then that is called *statutory rape*, and they can be prosecuted. If you have sex with someone who is under the age of 16, then you can be prosecuted.

If you and your partner are over the age of 16, then this is what consent is:

- A voluntary and enthusiastic 'yes' (it's more than just 'not saying no' – it has to be a 'yes').
- Informed (you know what you are saying 'yes' to).
- Not forced (if you only said 'yes' after being put under pressure, this is not consent).
- For some things and not others (if you consent to a kiss, that doesn't mean you have also consented to sex).
- Able to be withdrawn at any point (if you are having sex and you decide you don't want to do it anymore, you can and should stop).
- Not under the influence of alcohol or drugs (if someone is drunk or high to the point where they are slurring their words or stumbling around, they cannot give consent).
- Mandatory (your partner *must* get consent from you, and you *must* get consent from your partner).

Consent is all about communication, which many autistic people struggle with. So it's good to think about some things to say, so that you're prepared.

Good things to say if you don't want to do something (or if you want to stop doing something):

- 'No'
- 'No, thank you'
- 'I don't feel like it'
- 'I don't feel well'
- 'Stop'
- 'I don't want to do this anymore'
- 'That doesn't feel very nice'
- 'I'm not enjoying this.'

You do not have to give an explanation *why* you don't want to do something, but, if they keep asking and you want to get them to stop asking, 'I feel sick' or 'I don't feel well' can be useful.

Good things to say if you do want to do something (or if you want something to continue):

- 'Yes'
- 'Yes, please'
- 'I want this'
- 'Keep going'
- 'I really enjoy that'
- 'Don't stop'
- 'That feels really good!'

Consent isn't just about *you* giving consent. It's important that the person you are with gives you consent, and that you understand what they are telling you (verbally or non-verbally). Here are some things that you can say before or during sex to make sure that the person you are with is consenting:

- 'Is that okay?'
- 'Do you want this?'

- 'Does that feel good?'
- 'What do you want me to do?'
- 'Do you want me to [you can mention a specific thing here]'
- 'Are you having fun?'
- 'Do you want to keep going?'
- 'Let me know if you want me to stop.'

It's important to pay attention to the body language of the other person as well. This can be difficult to understand, so here are some things to look out for:

- Tensing up – if the person you are with tenses up their muscles, it might be a sign that they aren't enjoying it or that something hurts. If you think someone might be tensing up because something hurts, or because they don't want to continue, ask one of the questions we just looked at.
- Unusual noises – it's likely that your partner will make noises during sex, but it's important that you understand them. If you are unsure if a moan is a 'good' moan or a 'bad' moan, ask using one of the questions we just looked at. If they start making noises that you haven't heard them make before, or suddenly change the noises they are making, it might be a sign that they aren't enjoying it or that something hurts.
- Silence – some people are quiet when they have sex, but if they aren't making any noise it's worth checking to see if they are enjoying it (as you may struggle to know otherwise).
- If their vagina isn't very wet/penis isn't very hard, sometimes, this might happen because the person is

nervous, not because they don't want to have sex, but it's still a good idea to check and see whether they still want this and whether they are enjoying it (and what you can do to help them enjoy it more).

If you have more than one sexual experience with a person, it's a good idea to get to know their little 'quirks' when they have sex, so you can get better at interpreting what's going on. If you need to speak to them about it, don't be afraid to. If you need to ask them questions about what to look out for, don't be afraid to. And if you need to make notes, don't be afraid to. It might not sound 'sexy', but making sure your partner and you are having the best possible time is one of the sexiest things you can do.

If you struggle to communicate verbally, or are worried that you might not be able to remember to speak, then make sure you work out some sort of code with your partner beforehand. It could be some simple sign language for 'yes', 'no' or 'stop'. It could be to let them know that if you squeeze their arm in a certain way, something is hurting or you want to stop. It could be to have your phone with you so you can use text to communicate non-verbally what you want to happen or whether you want to stop.

Remember: sex isn't like it is in films, TV shows or porn. It can be messy, it can be awkward, you will have to check that things are going okay, and you are allowed to laugh if something is funny. It's likely there will be body fluids, it's likely that you might accidentally kick or elbow your partner, and your body might make strange noises. As long as you are both consenting, and both looking after each other, then you're doing great.

Having sex as an LGBTQIA+ person

As a young person, I was only ever taught about the 'cis man's penis going into a cis woman's vagina' sort of sex. I was not taught that there is an array of different ways to have sex, or that sex could happen between a vast combination of genders in a vast combination of ways.

So that's what we're going to look at now. It won't be a step-by-step 'how to' guide on how to have sex each way, but it will give you an idea of what you can do and, more importantly, how to be safe when you do it.

'P-in-V' (penis-in-vagina) sex

This is the kind of sex that you have probably learned about already. It's considered 'straight' sex, although not everyone with a penis is a man and not everyone with a vagina is a woman, so some LGBTQIA+ people do have this kind of sex. In P-in-V sex, someone with a penis will put their penis into someone else's vagina, and they will move together until one (or hopefully both!) reach orgasm.

Here's how to be safe and comfortable:

- Use a condom – this prevents pregnancy *and* the majority of sexually transmitted diseases (although external infections such as genital warts may still be passed on). Some condoms are ribbed (have bumps on them) or sometimes have a substance on them to make them feel tingly inside the vagina, so if you or your partner have sensory issues make sure that the condom you are using is comfortable for you both. Some people are also allergic to latex, and you can get latex-free condoms.

- Use another form of contraception (such as the pill, diaphragm, implant, injection or coil) – to ensure that you prevent pregnancy (you can find out more about different methods of contraception here: www.nhs.uk/ conditions/contraception).
- Use lubricant – use as much lubricant, or lube, as you need in order to be as comfortable as possible. The vagina does naturally lubricate itself, but there's nothing wrong with adding more lube – this doesn't mean you or your partner has failed. Some lube is flavoured, scented or made to create a 'tingly' sensation, so if you or your partner have sensory issues make sure that you are using a lube that is comfortable for you both.
- If you have a vagina, pee after sex – if you have a vagina, and your partner has a penis, and you have P-in-V sex, make sure that you go to the toilet straight after you finish sex. This will help to prevent urinary tract infections, which can be very, very painful.

Anal sex
This is the kind of sex that people often think about when they think of two men being together. It means that one person puts their penis in another person's anus (their bottom). Of course, not all men have penises, and not every person who has a penis is a man. If you have a vagina, and your partner has a penis (or the other way around) you might also enjoy anal sex. In the same way, some men who have sex with men may not like anal sex, so may choose other ways of having sex.

Here's how to be safe and comfortable:

- Use a condom – this prevents the majority of sexually transmitted diseases (although external infections such as genital warts may still be passed on). Some condoms are ribbed (have bumps on them) or sometimes have a substance on them to make them feel tingly, so if you or your partner have sensory issues make sure that the condom you are using is comfortable for you both. Some people are also allergic to latex, and you can get latex-free condoms.
- If you have a vagina, and are having anal sex with your partner who has a penis, use another form of contraception (such as the pill, diaphragm, implant, injection or coil). This might seem a bit strange, as you might think that pregnancy can only happen if the penis is in the vagina. While it is very unlikely for pregnancy to come from anal sex, it's a good idea to protect against it anyway – to ensure that you prevent pregnancy (you can find out more about different methods of contraception here: www.nhs.uk/conditions/contraception).
- Use lubricant – use as much lubricant, or lube, as you need in order to be as comfortable as possible. The rectum does not naturally lubricate like a vagina, so it's very important that you add lube. Some lube is flavoured, scented or made to create a 'tingly' sensation, so if you or your partner have sensory issues make sure that you are using a lube that is comfortable for you both.

Oral sex
There are a couple of different types of oral sex, but we'll look at them all in this paragraph. Essentially, oral sex is when one

partner uses their mouth – usually the lips and tongue – on their partner's genitals. This might mean putting your mouth on your partner's penis or vagina, and having your partner put their mouth on your penis or vagina. There's lots of different ways you can do this, or that you can experience it, but it all comes down to what feels good for you and what feels good for your partner. All different types of couples, of all different sexualities and genders, might enjoy oral sex.

Here's how to be safe and comfortable:

- Use a condom – if you are having oral sex that involves a penis (this is also called a 'blow job'), it's important to use a condom. This is because, although it's not as common, some sexually transmitted infections can be passed on through the mouth. Some condoms are ribbed (have bumps on them) or sometimes have a substance on them to make them feel tingly inside the vagina, which might feel very strange, uncomfortable or even painful, as the mouth is very sensitive. Make sure that the condom you are using is comfortable for you both.
- Use a dental dam – if you are having oral sex that involves a vagina (this is also called 'cunnilingus'), it's important to use a type of protection called a dental dam. This is like a condom, only it's a flat sheet that you spread over the area before putting your mouth on it. Some dental dams can be flavoured, so make sure that the one you are using is either a flavour that you like (you can't always tell by the packet, so try one out first) or doesn't have any flavour. Make sure that the dental dam you are using is comfortable for you both.

Fingering/Handjobs

This is when people use their hands and fingers on their partner's genitals in order to make them feel good. It might include putting your hand around someone's penis (also called a 'handjob'), or putting your fingers in their vagina or anus (also called 'fingering'). There's lots of things you can do with your hands, and neither you nor your partner will like everything that you can do, so it's important to communicate with each other to figure out what you like.

Here's how to be safe and comfortable:

- Wash your hands – although using your hands on your partner is a very safe form of sex, it's not completely safe. It's important to make sure you wash your hands well before doing it, to lower the risk of spreading infections and germs. If you move between touching your partner's anus and touching their vagina or penis, it's a good idea to wash your hands in between so you don't spread bacteria from one part of the body to another.

- Use protection – if washing your hands in this way seems like a bit much, you might want to use either condoms or dentals dams while fingering (using your hands on your partner's vagina or anus). Make sure you change to new ones if you move your hand to a different body part.

- Use lubricant – use as much lubricant, or lube, as you need in order to be as comfortable as possible. Some lube is scented or made to create a 'tingly' sensation, so if you or your partner have sensory issues make sure that you are using a lube that is comfortable for you both.

Sex toys

This is when people use specially designed sex toys (such as dildos and vibrators) to make either themselves or each other feel good. You can buy different types of toys, that can be used on different parts of the body. If you try one and don't like it, that's fine – it's all about what works for you. Lots of people, of different genders and sexualities, use and enjoy sex toys. Do *not* use regular objects you find in your house as sex toys – this could cause you serious harm. It's always best to buy especially made sex toys.

Here's how to be safe and comfortable:

- Wash your toys – it's important to make sure that any toys you are using are washed after every use, and are clean before you use them (if you haven't used it in a while, and you want to use it, it's worth giving it another clean before using it. If you are using the same toy in different parts of the body, such as in the anus and the vagina, make sure that you wash the toy thoroughly in between so you don't spread bacteria from one part of the body to another.

- Use a condom – if you are using a sex toy that goes inside the body (either in the vagina or anus) it's a good idea to use a condom on the toy to make sure that any bacteria on the toy doesn't end up in your body. Make sure you change to a new one if you start using the toy on a different body part.

- Use lubricant – use as much lubricant, or lube, as you need in order to be as comfortable as possible. Some lube is scented or made to create a 'tingly' sensation, so if you or your partner have sensory issues make sure that you are using a lube that is comfortable for you both.

Losing your virginity

If you haven't had sex, people may say that you are 'a virgin'.

When you have sex for the first time, many people call it 'losing your virginity'.

However, a lot of the common ideas about 'virginity' are based on a very heterosexual (straight) and cisgender idea of what sex is.

For example, if you have a vagina, and your partner has a penis, the first time that you have the kind of sex where they put their penis in your vagina would be considered 'losing your virginity'. But this can get very confusing, as there are lots of different types of ways to have sex: if you have a vagina, and your partner has a penis, are you still considered a virgin if you've done lots of the *other* types of sex acts but just *haven't* done the penis-in-vagina sex?

And if you have a penis and your partner has a penis, at what point is it said that you have 'lost your virginity'? If you have a vagina, and your partner has a vagina, what do you have to do before you are no longer considered a 'virgin'?

The more you think about it, the more confusing it seems to get!

But don't worry.

The reason for this confusion is that 'virginity' is what we call a social construct. This means that it is an idea that humans have made up, but it doesn't have a real, biological definition. Your body is the same, whether you have had sex, done any sort of sex acts, or not had any type of sex at all.

You may hear 'losing your virginity' referred to as 'popping your cherry'. This is because it was traditionally thought that the hymen, a protective little barrier stretched over the entrance of the vagina in people who have vaginas, breaks the first time a penis goes into the vagina. However, we now know that this isn't accurate.

The hymen can be different shapes and sizes for lots of different people. For some people, it may stretch a little the first time they have sex. It can also stretch, or even be torn, by exercise, bike riding, putting in a tampon or using a sex toy.

For many people, any type of sex for the first time might be uncomfortable, or even hurt. This might be because you are very nervous and tense, or it might be because you just need to get used to the feeling of it, or it might be because you just need to try having sex in a different way. Some people enjoy their first time. Some people don't. Whatever your experience, you are not doing it wrong.

Find out what works for you, use as much lube as you need (making sure it's the type of lube that doesn't make you uncomfortable), and make sure that you and your partner are comfortable and happy with what is happening. Foreplay, such as kissing and cuddling and touching, might also help to make your first time more relaxed and less uncomfortable.

Remember: your value is not changed based on whether you have or haven't had any type of sex. You are not 'broken' if you are in your twenties and haven't had any type of sex. You are not 'tainted' if you have had multiple sexual partners. And you are not more or less LGBTQIA+ depending on how much experience you have with sex.

Let's talk about rape and abuse

We've talked about the importance of consent, but we also need to talk about rape and sexual abuse.

If someone has sex with you or performs sex acts on you without your consent, then that is rape or sexual abuse. If you are under the age of 16, and someone older than 16 has sex with you or performs sex acts on you, then that is called statutory rape (as you are not old enough to give consent).

If someone has sex with you while you are under the influence of alcohol or drugs, and are much more impaired than they are (e.g. so drunk or high that you can't walk in a straight line, whereas they can), then that is rape or sexual assault.

It is also rape or sexual assault if someone who is caring for you has sex or performs a sex act on you. If you are in supported living, or have a carer of some description, and someone in that position does something sexual with you, that is not allowed (even if you are above the age of consent). They have a duty to look after you, and they are in a position of power – if they do something sexual with you, they have abused that power.

You might love the person who has done something sexual with you without your consent. You might be in a relationship with them. Or they might tell you that they love you, or that what is happening is 'normal'. They might try to convince you that you 'wanted it'. But it isn't okay.

If you are under the age of 16 and someone older than you is doing sexual things with you, that's rape or sexual assault.

If someone who is in a position of power over you, like a teacher or a carer, is doing sexual things with you, that's rape or sexual assault.

And you deserve to be protected.

If you are in a relationship with somebody and they persuade you to do things you don't want to do – for example, if they persuade you to have sex when you don't want to, and you have said clearly that you don't want to – then that is rape or sexual abuse. If you said no, and they then persuaded you to say 'yes' (even though you still didn't really want to), then that is rape or sexual abuse.

You do not *have* to have sex with someone because you are in a relationship with them. Who has sex with you, and what sex acts you perform or have performed on you, are *your* decision and no one else's. If somebody doesn't respect that and tries to do it anyway (or succeeds in making you say 'yes' instead) then they are abusive and they do not respect you.

People of all genders and all sexualities can commit rape and sexual assault. If you are a woman who has been raped or sexually abused by a woman, a man who has been raped or sexually abused by a man, or a man who has been raped or sexually abused by a woman, then your experiences are valid.

If you think you might have experienced rape, sexual assault or sexual abuse, don't be afraid to reach out and speak to someone. See 'Sexual abuse' in the 'More information' section at the end of the chapter for some organizations you can contact, and the different ways you can communicate with them.

In England, it is only legally called 'rape' if it involves someone putting their penis inside you without your consent. However, if you have been sexually assaulted by someone without a penis, or someone who used their fingers or other objects without your consent, you are absolutely allowed to say you have been raped. There are people working right now to challenge the legal definition of rape to reflect this.

More information

Books

Doing It! Let's Talk About Sex by Hannah Witton

Gender Identity, Sexuality and Autism by Eva A. Mendes and Meredith R. Maroney

LGBTQ: The Survival Guide for Lesbian, Gay, Bisexual, Transgender, and Questioning Teens by Kelly Huegel Madrone

The Pride Guide: A Guide to Sexual and Social Health for LGBTQ Youth by Jo Langford

Links

LGBT Foundation: http://lgbt.foundation/sexualhealth (although it is based in Manchester, the online advice is helpful)

clinicQ: https://cliniq.org.uk (a queer inclusive trans-led wellbeing and sexual health service)

Stonewall: www.stonewall.org.uk/category/sexual-health (a list of organizations and websites that might be helpful)

The National Autistic Society: www.autism.org.uk/sexeducation (this is aimed at parents and carers, but it still has some useful information)

Gendered Intelligence: http://genderedintelligence.co.uk/projects/kip/sexualhealth

Autism and Sexual Vulnerability – One Woman's Story, article on

Neuroclastic: https://neuroclastic.com/2019/11/22/autism-and-sexual-vulnerability-one-womans-story

No, Autistic People Are not Sexless, article by Violet Fenn: https://metro.co.uk/2018/01/10/no-autistic-people-are-not-sexless-our-sex-lives-are-as-varied-as-anyones-7141226

YouTube videos

The Sex Education You Never Had *PRIDE EDITION* by Ellbat: http://bit.do/Sex-Education-You-Never-Had
In this hour-long video, Ellbat (with an appearance by Fox Fisher) answers lots of questions about all things LGBTQIA+, including having sex as an LGBTQIA+ person. You can find the question you need answering, and what time they appear in the video, in the description box for easy access to information.

Disability, Sex, Relationships and Dating Roundtable by Hannah Witton: http://bit.do/Disability-Sex-Relationships-and-Dating
A roundtable hosted by Hannah Witton, featuring a frank and relaxed discussion with disabled people on their experiences with sex, relationships and dating. Hannah's channel is dedicated to talking about sex, relationships and disability – if there's something you want to know, Hannah will probably have a video on it! You can find her channel here: https://www.youtube.com/user/hannahgirasol.

Autism and Sexuality by Purple Ella: http://bit.do/Autism-And-Sexuality
A discussion about autism and sexuality, including how being autistic and having sensory issues can impact sex and relationships.

Sex; Trauma, Disabled and Autistic by Agony Autie: http://bit.do/Sex-Trauma-Disabled-Autistic

A very frank and personal discussion of one woman's experiences as a queer, disabled, autistic person navigating sex and trauma. It includes talking about sex after trauma, communicating with sexual partners and different ways of looking at sex. There are discussions of abuse, assault and trauma, so it comes with a trigger warning.

Sexual abuse

Galop – An organization supporting LGBTQIA+ people who have experienced hate crime, domestic abuse or sexual violence

Website:

- www.galop.org.uk

Phone:

- 020 7704 2040 (ask to speak to someone from the Sexual Violence Support Service)

Email:

- referrals@galop.org

Online form:

- www.galop.org.uk/report

Rape Crisis – A network of independent rape crisis centres for women and girls aged 16+ across the country

Website:

- https://rapecrisis.org.uk

Phone:

- 0808 802 9999 (open midday to 2.30pm, and 7pm to 9.30pm every day of the year)

Live chat:

- https://rapecrisis.org.uk/get-help/want-to-talk (Monday: 2pm to 4.30pm, 6pm to 9pm; Tuesday: 2pm to 4.30pm, 6pm to 9pm; Wednesday: 12pm to 2.30pm, 6pm to 9pm; Thursday: 12pm to 2.30pm, 6pm to 8.30pm; Friday: 9am to 11.30am)

Find a local rape crisis centre:

- https://rapecrisis.org.uk/get-help/find-a-rape-crisis-centre (note: these contact details only cover England and Wales. A list of similar resources for people outside England and Wales can be found

at: https://rapecrisis.org.uk/get-help/looking-for-information/
support-outside-of-england-wales)

Survivors UK – A service for male survivors of sexual abuse and rape. An
inclusive service for anyone who identifies as male, trans, non-binary, has
identified as male in the past, or anyone who feels that they are the right fit
for them

Phone:
- 0203 598 3898 (Monday to Friday, 9.30am to 5pm)

Email:
- help@survivorsuk.org

Online chat:
- www.survivorsuk.org/young-people/help-online (Monday to Sunday,
  midday to 8pm. When you contact them, they will also give you options
  to communicate through text or WhatsApp)

Childline – A counselling service for children and young people in the UK
provided by the NSPCC

Phone:
- 0800 1111 (free and open 24/7, although calls between midnight and
  7.30am may be limited to 15 minutes)
- There are some Welsh-speaking counsellors. When calling, let them
  know that you would like to speak to someone in Welsh and a time will
  be arranged for you to do this

Online chat:
- www.childline.org.uk/get-support/1-2-1-counsellor-chat (click the box
  on the right-hand side to enter the waiting room. There is a traffic light
  system to indicate how busy the service is, and how long you might have
  to wait)

Art box:
- www.childline.org.uk/toolbox/art-box (this enables you to draw about
  how you are feeling. If you struggle to express yourself with words, or
  English isn't your first language, you can share what you draw with the
  counsellor you speak to in the online chat)
- You will need to create an account and sign in to save what you draw.
  You can do this by clicking on the box in the bottom right hand corner
  next to the Art box

Message boards:
- www.childline.org.uk/get-support/message-boards (you can chat with
  other young people who understand or may have gone through the same
  thing)

CHAPTER 8

Out and About: LGBTQIA+ Spaces

The LGBTQIA+ community has been around for a very long time. Throughout history, LGBTQIA+ people have found their own spaces, where they can be themselves, with each other, and be safe being who they are.

In recent history, these spaces have been mainly bars and clubs. The Stonewall Riots, which many people see as the trigger for the LGBTQIA+ rights movement, took place after the Stonewall Inn, a pub, was raided by the police.

Although LGBTQIA+ community spaces are much more visible these days, bars and clubs continue to be the centre of what is called the 'gay scene'. They are still very important for the community. You have gay bars, lesbian bars, large nightclubs, clubs that focus on drag performances, and other bars and clubs of different sizes, atmospheres, and busyness.

I first tried to enter the community scene as a university student. I had only been to nightclubs a few times before then, as I found them overwhelming due to the noise, the lights, and the numbers of people. I also found it very tricky being around drunk people, as it was even more difficult than normal to predict what they were going to do. However, I had never been to a gay club before and decided to see what they were like.

Unfortunately, I had the same sensory and anxiety issues in gay clubs as I had had in the 'normal' clubs back home. As a young bisexual woman, who was already very insecure about whether she belonged in the community, this was very hard to deal with. I felt very cut off from other people like me.

When it came to finding my place in the community, it took a little more time and a little more searching before I found spaces that weren't so overwhelming. I'll be going over how to do this and what to look for later in this chapter.

Not every autistic person will have the same experiences as me. Some autistic people are sensory seekers and can thrive in spaces like nightclubs. Other autistic people may be more able to deal with it, or may want to go to these places but need some advice on how to cope.

Because of this, we'll also look at the more traditional LGBTQIA+ spaces, what you might experience in them, and how to cope in them if you struggle with noise, lighting or large crowds.

Note: often people will say 'gay club' and 'gay bar' as if they are the same thing. You might hear someone say a place is a 'gay bar', and then when you arrive it might be more like a club. We'll be looking at the two separately, but it's a good idea to double check whether somewhere is a club or a bar before you go.

Traditional venues

Gay clubs
This is the first thing that comes to mind for most people when they think of an LGBTQIA+ space. Although you will hear them called 'gay clubs', they can also be safe spaces for people who don't identify as 'gay'. It's often a good idea to ask online, particularly in local Facebook groups, to find out more about which clubs in your area are safest for your particular identity (sexuality and gender).

If you search for LGBTQIA+ spaces, you will likely be directed towards a gay club. There are probably more gay clubs (and gay bars) than any other LGBTQIA+ venue.

Gay clubs will often be quite busy and quite dark, with very bright (sometimes flashing) lights. There will also likely be people who are drunk or who are drinking alcohol. Gay clubs are mainly night-time venues, where people go to dance and to drink, so the music will probably be very loud (often with a thumping beat).

Some gay clubs may have quieter rooms or spaces, so you may want to get in touch with a venue beforehand to see if it has a more accessible space if you need it (or you can get someone else to do this for you).

Gay bars
Gay bars are similar to gay clubs – they are places for people to meet, often in the evening, and can get very busy. However, they are a little bit quieter. While clubs revolve around loud music and dancing, bars are more about spending time with other people and drinking.

It's often a good idea to ask online, particularly in local Facebook groups, to find out more about which bars in your area are safest for your particular identity (sexuality and gender).

The music is likely to be quieter (although it can still be loud) than in a club, and the lights a little bit less overwhelming. There may even be performances, such as bands, singers or drag shows (there are also bars dedicated to drag shows, which we'll talk about later on). Some gay bars have karaoke nights or quiz nights, so it's a good idea to look up what is going on.

However, bars have a big focus on alcohol, so there is likely to be a lot of drunk people and some pressure to drink. If this makes you uncomfortable, or if you know that you have a problem with alcohol, it's a good idea to think about whether a bar (or a club) is safe for you.

If you want to have a night out but can't quite cope with how loud or bright a gay club is, a gay bar might be the right place for you.

Some gay bars will also be open during the day. Many might serve food, if you want to meet up for lunch in an LGBTQIA+ friendly place.

Some gay bars may have quieter rooms or spaces, so you may want to get in touch with a venue beforehand to see if it has a more accessible space if you need it (or you can get someone else to do this for you).

Lesbian bars
Lesbian bars are very similar to gay bars, but they are aimed at LGBTQIA+ women.

Although they are called 'lesbian bars', they can be a safe space for any LGBTQIA+ people who identify as women or with women (e.g. some trans-masculine people may not be women, but they may identify as lesbians or feel safer in these spaces). It's often a good idea to ask online, particularly in local Facebook groups, to find out more about which bars in your area are safest for your particular identity (sexuality and gender).

Like gay bars, lesbian bars are likely to be quieter (although they can still be loud) than a club, and the lights a little bit less overwhelming. There may even be performances, such as bands, singers or drag shows (there are also bars dedicated to drag shows, which we'll talk about later on). Some lesbian bars have karaoke nights or quiz nights, so it's a good idea to look up what is going on.

However, bars have a big focus on alcohol, so there is likely to be a lot of drunk people and some pressure to drink. If this makes you uncomfortable, or if you know that you have a problem with alcohol, it's a good idea to think about whether a bar (or a club) is safe for you.

If you identify either as a woman or with women, and feel safer around other others who identify as women or with women, a lesbian bar might be the right place for you.

As with other types of bars, some lesbian bars may have quieter rooms or spaces, so you could contact a venue beforehand to see if it has a more accessible space if you need it (or you can get someone else to do this for you).

Drag bars
Drag bars are similar to gay and lesbian bars, with the difference being that they are focused around drag performances. People will mainly go to these bars to see a drag show.

Drag is when performers perform as a certain gender in an over-exaggerated way. There are drag queens, where people (often cis men, but not always), perform as women, and there are drag kings, where people (often cis women, but not always) perform as men. Their performances may include singing, dancing, lip-synching to songs, and interacting with the audience.

Many drag bars involve audience participation, so if this makes you anxious, it may be best to avoid them (or find out where best to sit to avoid being picked out of the crowd).

Not all drag bars are the same. Some may be louder, some may be more sexy, some may encourage performers with a darker or more offensive sense of humour. This is why it's important to do some research beforehand, to make sure that you're comfortable with the tone of the show. If there are any YouTube videos from the bar, have a watch of these beforehand.

Different drag bars are run by different people with different attitudes towards people of all genders and sexualities. As with other spaces, it's often a good idea to ask online, particularly in local Facebook groups, to find out more about which clubs in your area are safest for your particular identity (sexuality and gender).

At some bars, there may be a number of drunk people and some pressure to drink. If this makes you uncomfortable, or if you know that you have a problem with alcohol, it's a good idea to think about whether a bar is safe for you.

If you want a bar with quieter rooms or spaces, get in touch with the venue beforehand to see if it has a more accessible space if you need it (or get someone else to do this for you).

Quieter spaces

While there was a time when bars and clubs were the main spaces for LGBTQIA+ people to find their community, we are lucky that there are now alternative quieter spaces that you might want to take advantage of.

Youth groups

LGBTQIA+ youth groups are a great space for young people to make friends, socialize, and be around people who understand them. They are also often supervised by an adult, so you may feel safer being in that sort of space.

Youth groups may do a lot of different things: sitting and chatting, arts and crafts, trips, activities, learning about LGBTQIA+ history, support on a specific issue (figuring out your sexuality or gender identity, coming out, problems at work, discrimination etc.) or campaigning and activism in your local community. It's important to find what you are comfortable with, and communicate that to the group leaders (by speaking to them, by text, or by email or letter) so they can make sure you're only taking part in the kind of things you feel safe to take part in.

You don't have to be absolutely certain of your identity in order to join a youth group. If you are questioning your sexuality or your gender, a local youth group may be a safe space for you to meet other people in the community and figure out what fits you best.

There are several ways that you can find out if your area has an LGBTQIA+ youth group that you can attend. The Proud Trust runs youth groups in the north of England, but has a special search engine that you can use to find other LGBTQIA+ groups in your area: www. theproudtrust.org/for-young-people/lgbt-youth-groups/ where-can-i-find-a-youth-group.

If you can't find a local group using The Proud Trust

website, you might have more luck with googling your local area and 'LGBTQIA+ youth group' to see if anything comes up.

If you live in a more rural or isolated area, there might not be any groups active near you. If you can't find anything, you might want to look at setting up your own group. Remember that you don't *have* to do this. But, if you do, Stonewall has put together a guide to setting up LGBTQIA+ youth groups: www.stonewall.org.uk/setting-lgbt-youth-group.

If you don't feel able to set up your own group, you can still find some support, either through other LGBTQIA+ groups or through online communities.

If you do find a youth group local to you, bear in mind that they may not have come into direct contact with autistic people (that they know of), so you might want to direct them to some further information about autism and autistic people.

University groups

If you live in a town that has a university, or near a town that has a university, then it's very likely that there will be an LGBTQIA+ group at that university. When I was at university, the LGBTQIA+ Association was my introduction to the community, and where I found my first group of 'real life' friends in the community.

You don't have to go to the university in order to look into this. If you look into whether your local university has an LGBTQIA+ group, you should be able to get in touch with them and ask if you can attend some of their events.

University LGBTQIA+ groups will have a number of activities that happen throughout the week. There may be some events that involve going to clubs and bars. You might feel safer going to one of these spaces with a group like this (especially if you follow some of the advice I'll be giving at the end of the chapter).

Many university LGBTQIA+ groups will host coffee mornings, breakfasts or lunches, which are a lot quieter than bars and clubs. If you struggle with talking to people in a setting like this, many of these groups will also hold events like quizzes, where you can get to know people through doing an activity.

Remember that university groups like this are run by young people (even if they are slightly older than you) with shared experiences around sexuality and gender. Don't be afraid to reach out to the organizers of these groups, explain any fears you have (crowds, meeting new people etc.) and what might help you to attend.

They may not have come into direct contact with autistic people (that they know of), so you might want to direct them to some further information about autism and autistic people.

'Older' LGBTQIA+ groups

In my experience, groups that are made up of 'older' members of the LGBTQIA+ community may be slightly quieter or easier for an autistic person to cope with.

After my mum came out in her middle age, she attended and now helps to run a group for women who love women; this mainly takes the form of coffee mornings and an online group where they can chat, support one another, and spend time with people who understand.

If you can find one of these, you may find it a more comfortable environment than younger LGBTQIA+ spaces, which may be more focused around going out and doing activities.

These groups may also arrange outings to bars and clubs,

and, as with university groups, you might feel safer and more able to go to these places with a group of people you trust.

However, as these groups consist mainly of adults, who are likely to be quite a bit older than you, make sure that you are safe and supported within the group. If you have any concerns about anyone within the group, please find someone to speak to. Don't be afraid to speak to the group leaders about your concerns.

Pride

When people think of the LGBTQIA+ community, one of the first things that comes to mind is the annual Pride celebrations. But Pride can take many different forms, so it's important to have a look and see which ones might make you more comfortable.

Big Pride parades

Most major cities will have some sort of Pride celebration, and the key part of those celebrations will be the Pride parade. This is a parade that goes through the city centre and celebrates lots of different groups and organizations that are a part of the LGBTQIA+ community. It's often very colourful, very happy and very loud.

Pride parades can be an amazing experience, but they can also be overwhelming. The parade has spectators along the route, and the crowds can get very big and people can be very squashed together. If you are in a big city, it's unlikely you will be able to watch the Pride parade without being in the middle of a crowd (meaning that people will be bumping into you and touching you).

If you are in the parade, there will be a lot of music, a lot of people, and lots of cheering and colours.

Big Pride parades are an amazing thing, but you might have to make a plan for what to do if you go and it becomes too much. Make sure you take a phone charger with you if you go with friends, so you always have charge on your phone to find them if you get separated.

There will be more suggestions on ways to navigate queer spaces as an autistic person in a few pages' time.

Big Pride events

Outside the Pride parades, big cities will often hold a large event to celebrate Pride. This will probably be in the form of some sort of festival in a field or in a park, and may include a stage with performances. In cities like Manchester and Brighton, there might even be performances from big stars like Lady Gaga or Britney Spears.

Unlike the parade, these events may have quieter spaces. There are often places selling things, and places to buy food and drinks, and some of these areas might be a good place to sit down and recharge. However, there is no guarantee of this, as these events can get incredibly crowded (particularly if a big star is performing).

It's likely that there will be drinking at these events, and there may be tents dedicated to partying and drinking. If you are planning to go to one of these big events, you might want to get in touch with the organizer beforehand to find out if there are any planned quiet or safe spaces for the event. You might also want to request a plan of the event, so you know where to go and what to avoid.

It's also worth noting that it can cost a lot of money to get into one of these events, so you want to be absolutely certain that you will be okay (you don't want to have to leave early and waste all that money).

Smaller Pride parades/events

If the big Pride parades/events in the big cities sound a bit too overwhelming, you might want to look into one of the many small local Pride parades/events that take place across the country.

Small local Prides will often involve a walking parade through the town centre, with a few hundred people taking part in the parade, that then ends in a reasonably sized festival/fete-type set-up in a park or a field. Although there may be some dedicated areas for drinking, and a stage with performances, it's likely to be a lot less crowded and a lot less loud than the bigger events.

As someone who does struggle with the noise and crowds of large events, I find the local Pride parades/events near me much more accessible. They are a lot quieter, a lot less hectic, and a lot less crowded. However, these can also get overwhelming for me after a while, so I make sure I have a plan in place with the people I'm going with. You can find out more about the techniques and plans I use to navigate these events a little further on in the chapter.

Local Pride events often have their own social media pages and are organized by the local council. They are therefore easier to get in touch with, so do ask them about any potential safe or quiet spaces that they could direct you towards. If you want to, you could offer to work with the local Pride organizers to make sure that there is a quiet space available for autistic people.

Other Pride events

When people think of Pride, they will normally think of the parades and the big event after the parade. However, there are Pride events happening in lots of different venues, in lots of different ways, and at lots of different times.

Some local areas will hold different Pride events over the course of a week. Individual LGBTQIA+ organizations may hold their own Pride-themed events. LGBTQIA+ venues like clubs and bars might also put on their own Pride events.

Some of the things you might see happening around Pride include:

- Quiz nights
- Coffee mornings
- Art exhibitions
- Karaoke nights
- Club nights
- Film nights
- Performances.

There is a lot to choose from if you start looking! It's good to have a look at social media for potential events in your area. There's very often enough going on for you to be able to find something you're comfortable with.

If you're not sure what an event might entail, or how accessible it will be for you as an autistic person, you can get in touch with the organizers to find out what to expect. You can then ask them if they will have any quiet or safe spaces during the event.

UK Black Pride

Pride celebrations in the UK have often been seen as an

incredibly white event, with LGBTQIA+ people of colour raising concerns about racism they have faced in the community. Because of this, UK Black Pride was started in 2005. It is Europe's largest celebration for African, Asian, Middle Eastern, Latin American and Caribbean heritage LGBTQIA+ people, attracting nearly 8000 people annually.

If you are an LGBTQIA+ person of colour who does not feel comfortable at Pride, UK Black Pride might be an important alternative for you. We know that mainstream LGBTQIA+ and disability communities are dominated by white people, and many people of colour have spoken about how UK Black Pride is a much safer space for them to celebrate Pride.

If you are an autistic LGBTQIA+ person of colour, UK Black Pride might be a fantastic place to celebrate all aspects of who you are, in a way that the more 'mainstream' Prides might not allow.

As with other Prides, it involves a stage, performances and places to buy things, food and drinks, and some of these areas might be a good place to sit down and recharge. It is a busy event, so could get crowded and noisy – you might want to get in touch with the organizer beforehand to find out if there are any planned quiet or safe spaces for the event. You might also want to request a plan of the event, so you know where to go and what to avoid (such as bars or spaces that might be louder).

If you are white and are considering attending UK Black Pride, do be aware that this is not an event that has been put on for you. If you attend, you attend as an ally, and you must step back and allow people of colour to take centre stage throughout.

Virtual Pride

As a result of the Covid-19 pandemic in 2020, most Pride celebrations in the UK were cancelled. However, one of the upsides to this for many disabled people was that some organizations moved their Pride celebrations online.

For example, talks and panels on different issues within the LGBTQIA+ community were carried out via online communications systems (such as Zoom, Microsoft Teams and Skype). A great example of this was Bi Pride UK, which launched the day-long virtual Bi-Fi Festival having had to cancel their event (you can find out more here: https://biprideuk.org/events).

Similarly, karaoke nights, quizzes and even club nights were also held in this way. These allowed people to connect with each other without leaving the house.

If you are someone who struggles with a loud or crowded environment, then these types of Pride events may be perfect. Having many of these events online certainly helped me to access Pride in a way I had never been able to before.

Although there is no knowing, at this point, whether virtual Pride celebrations will be carried on once the Covid-19 pandemic has run its course, Summer 2020 proved for many people that it is possible. Many LGBTQIA+ disabled people, including LGBTQIA+ autistic people, are calling for these events to become an annual thing.

Search for 'Virtual Pride' online to find out more about what went on in Summer 2020, and to keep up to date with whether these events will be carrying on into 2021 and beyond. You might even want to get in touch with your local Pride organizers to tell them what a Virtual Pride would mean to you.

Obviously, Virtual Pride is online, so you must be careful.

There will be more information on staying safe online at the end of this chapter.

Navigating LGBTQIA+ spaces as an autistic person

For autistic people, social situations can sometimes be a bit of a struggle. But, like me, you may still want to try to find a place for yourself in LGBTQIA+ spaces (whichever space you prefer). So here are some steps that I take to make sure that I am as safe and as comfortable as possible.

Have a way out
It's not the most joyful or optimistic thing to think about when you're preparing for some time out with friends. But once I've done it, the knowledge that I have a back-up plan always makes for a less stressful evening. Having a way out could be as simple as making sure you have several different routes to get home (printing it out as well, in case of phone problems), or as pre-planned as having written and rehearsed scripts on what to say when you want to leave. Good scripts, I've found, begin with 'I've had a really nice time, but...' and can be followed with:

- 'I have someone I need to pick up.'
- '(Insert family member here) needs my help.'
- 'I have tickets for a certain train.'
- 'I'm not feeling great.'
- 'I have work/school/an appointment early tomorrow morning.'
- Or simply – 'I have to go now.'

The closer to the actual truth the better, but if you have to embellish, a good rehearsal with a family member or trusted friend can be really helpful.

Have a 'buddy' code
Before going out, I'll make sure that I have at least one person that I trust enough to come up with a 'buddy' code. I'll speak to this person beforehand, outlining exactly what's making me anxious about the event (recently, for example, I reached out to a close friend and explained that I was extremely anxious at the thought of everyone getting drunk around me), the signs to look out for in case I struggle to communicate (hand signs, specific stimming, a code word or phrase, or a text), and what to do when those signs appear. Before I had a trusted friend for these things, I would have my mum as my 'buddy', and our code was 'I feel sick'. I would call or text, tell her I was feeling unwell, and she would hop in the car to come and collect me.

Use the toilet
The first thing I do when I get to a venue is work out where the toilets are. As pubs and bars can get loud and busy, the toilet is the perfect place to lock yourself in your own space for as long as you need to. This is where I go to catch my breath and recharge my batteries. Toilets in these places can also get crowded and noisy, but they will be less so than the main area, and you can lock yourself into a cubicle to create a safe space where you can stim, put your headphones on, or simply do some breathing exercises until you feel ready to face the world. Plus, no one will question you going to the toilet, and they will very rarely notice or question how long you take.

Set your limits and be firm

Set a clear limit with yourself and others: I will only stay until a certain time, if people move on to a certain club I won't go with them, here is a list of things that make me uncomfortable and that I will not do, and so on. Write these down to remind yourself. If you feel comfortable doing so, let the other people in your group know where your boundaries are. If you don't feel comfortable doing so, ask your buddy to mention it – buddies can also be important tools in making sure you stick to your limits and stand firm against anyone who tries to get you to cross them.

Use your techniques

If, like me, you have some idea of what helps to calm you down, make sure you have a list of these to hand (printed, written down, on your phone etc.). Those same ideas apply here, and in many other situations. These techniques and strategies may include:

- Stimming aids – fidget spinners, fidget cubes, soft toys, chewable jewellery, a heavy scarf. Have a play around and see what works for you. Chewable jewellery, fidget toys and scarves can be found for ridiculously good prices on Amazon, and you can also get lovely little soft toys of various textures that fit neatly in the bottom of your bag.
- Breathing – my favourite calming breathing exercise is the 4–7–8 technique: breathe in for four seconds, hold for seven seconds, and breathe out for eight seconds. It works for me, but make sure you look it up beforehand so you know how to do it effectively and safely (www.youtube.com/watch?v=YRPh_GaiL8s). If

other techniques work better for you, don't be afraid to do these either. Write them down if you have to, and don't forget that the magic toilet cubicle safe space is there for you to use if you need it.

- Headphones – if you have some noise-cancelling head-phones, don't be afraid to put them on. Depending on whether they are bluetooth enabled or not, you could also pop some calming sounds on without getting too tied up with wires in a public place. My favourite soundscapes for these moments can be found on myNoise (https://mynoise.net), which also has an app that you can download for when you don't have a good internet signal.

- Apps – there are loads of apps that could be helpful here. Whether it's a meditation app (there are a *lot* of these, and it's about finding which ones work for you), a gaming app, a fidget app (to keep your hands and your brain distracted and away from the panic) or something entirely different, have a good search for whatever works best for you.

Don't feel guilty

Whatever happens, don't let what you have to do weigh on your conscience. I've been there, and it does no good for anybody. If you need to hide in the bathroom for 20 minutes, or put on your headphones for a little bit, or even if you have to leave earlier than planned, do not let yourself be dragged down by the thought that you are disappointing your friends. They may well be disappointed, but if they are the kind of friends every person deserves to have, they will understand. The very fact that you have made the effort to be there, in a situation which does not come naturally to you and for which you have to put a lot of systems in place, shows that you care about them.

If you can't go, you can't go
You have to be the judge of your own abilities. If it's been an awful day, if you feel on the edge, if you have no emotional energy, if you feel in your gut that going would be a bad idea, don't be afraid to back out. As much as it is important to regulate your own anxiety in order to take part in these situations and spend time with your friends, it is also imperative to remember to regulate your anxiety for your own wellbeing. If you are worried about upsetting your friends, talk to them if you can, or, if you feel you can't, ask your buddy to do so, write them an email, or send them a text. They may be more open to understanding than you think.

Online spaces

If you aren't comfortable in social situations, or if you aren't able to mentally or physically step outside as often as you would like, this doesn't mean you have to feel cut off from the community.

I have found great comfort, and a great sense of the community, in online spaces such as forums and social media.

Facebook
There are both open and closed LGBTQIA+ groups on Facebook (open meaning everyone can see what you post, closed meaning that you'll need to request to become a member and what you post will only be seen by other members). You can decide what works best for you (e.g. if you aren't out to all your friends and family yet, you may prefer a closed group).

There are rules on Facebook about using your legal name, so it's harder to be anonymous. It may also cause problems if you have socially changed your name, but have not legally changed your name, and Facebook may insist that you use your legal name.

You can also amend your settings on Facebook so that only people you are friends with can see your personal posts. You can also amend your settings so that specific posts can only be seen by specific friends.

Twitter

The best place to find community and support on Twitter is through hashtags. If you are looking to speak to other autistic people in the LGBTQIA+ community, you can use hashtags like #AskingAutistics, #ActuallyAutistic or #AllAutistics and say that you are specifically looking to connect with other LGBTQIA+ people.

You are able to be more anonymous on Twitter, and your username and profile do not have to reflect your legal name. You can use a completely made up name, or you can use your preferred name (if it's different to your legal name) and this shouldn't cause any problems.

You can also amend your settings on Twitter so that your tweets can only be seen by 'mutuals' (people who you follow who also follow you) or so that people have to request to see your timeline. However, bear in mind that going private means that tweeting with hashtags will only be seen by those who follow you.

Tumblr

This is a good place to find a community while remaining anonymous. It allows for more in terms of writing and responding to people than Twitter (which has a character limit) and allows you to put as little information in your username or profile as you want.

Tumblr is also a good place to share your thoughts, whether by blogging about them or through your artwork or through some other creative thing you do. People may respond to your experiences and thoughts, people may recognize what you're talking about, and that may become a bridge to being part of that community.

You can amend your privacy settings on Tumblr, hiding access to your email address and stopping your blog from appearing in certain searches on the site. You can also make your direct messages private, so you aren't contacted by strangers.

Forums

Forums, specifically around a certain topic, can be a great place to find a community and chat to others about your experiences.

There is an LGBTQIA+ specific forum that you can find at www.lgbtchat.net. It covers lots of different topics, including figuring stuff out, coming out and general everyday issues people are facing within the community.

If you have a special interest (such as being in a fandom, liking a band, enjoying a certain kind of sport or having an interest in railways), you may be able to find other people in the LGBTQIA+ community in a forum dedicated to that thing. You can then connect with them over a special interest. This is how I met many of my oldest friends, and a large part of how I found a place for myself in the LGBTQIA+ community.

Most forums allow you some degree of anonymity, and will let you set your privacy settings so you can manage who you talk to and when you talk to them. Most forums also have moderators, who will monitor posts and make sure that the forum is free from abuse and bullying. Make sure that you get in touch with these moderators if you have any concerns or anxieties about posting.

Staying safe in online LGBTQIA+ spaces as an autistic person

While online LGBTQIA+ spaces can be extremely important and helpful for us, as autistic people, it's also incredibly important that we are aware of the risks and make sure that we are safe. Here are a few tips, based on my experiences and on professional advice.

Don't share personal information
It's important that you don't share information such as your surname, address, email address, phone number and so on while communicating with others online. If it could be used to trace you and find out where you live or where you go to school, avoid publicly giving it out online. If you are figuring out your gender and/or sexuality with other people online, you may be tempted to share more personal details (such as medical details and sexual history). Make sure that you are very, very careful with this, and be as vague as you possibly can. If you are in any way uncertain about whether what you are saying is too much, it's best *not* to post it.

Don't believe everything you read online
It's very easy for people to lie on the internet. Although you will meet some people you really click with, it's important to remember that not everyone online is who they say they

are. Keep in mind that anyone can say they are anyone online. This also applies to things that people say. If someone says that something is fact, always make sure you check it before believing it. There are a lot of people on the internet who will try to divide the LGBTQIA+ community by spreading half-truths or outright lies (often targeting trans people and ace people). For example, if somebody says that bisexuality definitely means 'attraction to two genders', make sure you read up about it first before believing it – in this case, that hasn't been the definition of bisexuality for decades, but people saying it online can make other people believe it.

If you are uncomfortable, shut it down
If anybody you're communicating with online asks you to do anything that makes you uncomfortable, make sure that you block them and report them (each site will have different ways of reporting behaviour, so make sure you find out how to block and report before you start using that site). This might include the following things:

- Asking you to send naked or partially naked photos. This might also include asking for pictures of specific parts of your body, or of you dressed in a certain way or in certain clothes. If someone asks this, let somebody in authority know – if you are under the age of 18, asking you for naked photos is a crime and it needs to be reported.
- Asking you to get involved with anything involving drugs. Autistic people are sometimes pulled into things like drug smuggling, because we can be very trusting by nature. If someone asks you to do anything like this, report it. They do not have your best interests at heart.

- Talking about things that sound a bit extreme. This may include extreme religious ideas, or political ideas, and may target a specific group of people (e.g. they may talk about Muslims as if they are a threat to you). As autistic people, we are often susceptible to what they call 'radicalization', where we get drawn in by extremists with dangerous points of view. Always be on the lookout, particularly if they start talking about violence. As above, they don't have your best interests at heart.

You don't have to talk to anyone that you don't want to talk to. If someone continues to contact you when you ask them not to, make sure you continue to report them, and ask someone you trust for support.

Be kind, and expect kindness

Cyberbullying is a huge problem online, and many autistic people find themselves the victims. If you are autistic *and* LGBTQIA+, then there is a likelihood that someone on the internet will try and be mean to you about it. Remember that the people you are talking to online are real people, and that words can be very powerful. Be as kind as you can. However, if someone is being unkind to you, you don't have to try to reason with them or defend yourself – it's best to stop engaging, block them and report it to the site or the forum moderators. Being kind to others doesn't have to mean letting other people be unkind to you. You are important and you don't deserve that.

You can find out even more about how to stay safe in online spaces at: www.childnet.com.

Remember: there are many different ways to get involved in the LGBTQIA+ community, so don't force yourself into situations that make you uncomfortable. Even if it's just a few people you can safely share your experiences with, that counts! And once you start looking to speak to other autistic LGBTQIA+ people, you'll be amazed at how many there are.

More information

Books

LGBTQ: The Survival Guide for Lesbian, Gay, Bisexual, Transgender, and Questioning Teens by Kelly Huegel Madrone

Links

Stonewall: www.stonewall.org.uk/category/youth-groups (list of groups for young LGBTQIA+ people)

Gendered Intelligence: http://genderedintelligence.co.uk/projects/kip/transidentities/orgs (list of groups for young trans people)

LGBT Chat: www.lgbtchat.net

YouTube videos

Does Pride Exclude Disabled People? by Jessica Kellgren-Fozard: http://bit.do/Does-Pride-Exclude-Disabled-People
In this video, Jessica discusses the issues that disabled people can face at Pride and at Pride events, as well as the issues disabled people can face trying to find community groups and events. She also discusses ways in which LGBTQIA+ spaces can do better to include disabled people.

Making Queer Spaces Accessible by The AmBIssadors: http://bit.do/
Making-Queer-Spaces-Accessible
I am a guest in this video, talking with two other bisexual activists
about how we can make LGBTQIA+ spaces more accessible for
autistic people (as well as more accessible for other disabled people).

CHAPTER 9

Dealing with Bullying, Bigotry and Injustice

This is a bit of a bleak note to end on, but it's so important to talk about it. At the end of the chapter, we'll talk about ways you can get involved with positivity, activism and advocacy – so it's not all upsetting!

Not everyone in the world likes LGBTQIA+ people. Not everyone in the world likes autistic people. There are a lot of things that people say and people do that can be hateful and hurtful to us. Sometimes, people even try to find ways to harm us or other people in our community.

As autistic people, dealing with hate and bigotry and injustice can be even more difficult. We often find it difficult to filter our emotions. We often have strong views on right and wrong, and find injustice physically painful to see and deal with. As LGBTQIA+ autistic people, the anxiety and frustration of living in a world that doesn't always accept us can be overwhelming.

You deserve to protect yourself, to have boundaries, and to make sure you create safe spaces for yourself away from the unfairness in the world.

Bullying

A large number of autistic people will experience bullying at some point in their lives. A large number of LGBTQIA+ people will also experience bullying at some point in their lives. Although it can be particularly nasty at school, bullying can continue in the workplace.

Bullying might take the form of:

- calling you names (particularly slurs about your sexuality or your autism)
- deliberately misgendering you (using the wrong pronouns, using your old name after you've changed it etc.)
- making fun of you
- talking about you behind your back (especially if they make it clear that they are talking about you, but you don't know exactly what they're saying)
- threatening to hurt you
- stealing things from you
- hurting you (pushing, hitting, kicking, pinching, throwing things at you etc.).

There are a couple of different ways that you can respond to bullying.

Ignoring it
This is really difficult to do. I have a particularly hard time

doing this, and have very rarely been successful. However, it might work for you.

Many bullies do horrible things in order to get a reaction, so sometimes ignoring them can be the best way to make them stop. You won't necessarily know if this is true for your bully until you try it. If someone calls you a name, or makes fun of you, try pretending you didn't hear or just walking away without saying anything. If someone writes something nasty about you (like sticking things in your bag or on your locker), scrunch or tear it up and then put it in the bin. Doing something you enjoy, like reading, spending time with your friends, watching a film, playing games or doing something related to one of your interests can also be really helpful to take your mind away from what has been said or done.

If you are unable to ignore it, but don't want to publicly react to it, it might be useful to talk about it with someone you trust, either in person, through text or online. Let yourself cry about it or shout about it with someone you feel safe with.

If you don't feel comfortable with this, try keeping a journal – this can be written by hand, or on your phone, or on a private anonymous social media account. If it's on a bit of paper, tearing it up and throwing it in the bin can be really cathartic.

Of course, you might find that none of this works for you. It didn't work for me! You haven't failed if it doesn't work.

If someone is causing you real harm – triggering your dysphoria, damaging your mental health, stealing things from you or physically hurting you (or threatening to hurt you) – then it might not be a good idea to try to ignore it. For your own safety and wellbeing, it's important that you speak up.

Speaking out

When I say 'speak out', it doesn't necessarily have to be with your words. There are lots of ways that you can speak up, even if you don't speak or can't speak in moments like this. By 'speak out', I mean 'let someone know'.

If you are in school, this might be a teacher, a teaching assistant, or your parent or guardian. It might be an older student with some authority, like a prefect. You, or someone you trust, may want to email someone to let them know that something is going on. Or, if you feel able to, you might want to approach them directly after someone says something nasty to you.

If you are at work, you might reach out to a colleague, your manager, another manager that you trust, or go straight to someone in your company's Human Resources team. Like with school, you, or someone you trust, may want to email one of these people to let them know what's going on. It's a good idea to make a note of everything that happens, as it happens. This can be really helpful for dealing with it.

However, if you do speak out, there is not always a guarantee that the situation will be dealt with. This doesn't mean that you shouldn't speak out but you need to be aware that, sometimes, people with the power to help you might not help you.

Some people in power (teachers, managers, parents) can also be bullies. They might even be the ones who are bullying you – or they might not be willing to help you. You are not alone if this is the case.

If you speak out and the people you speak out to don't help you, you might want to look at getting away from the situation. If you are in school, this might mean speaking to someone you trust (such as your parent or guardian) about moving schools. If you are at work, this might mean looking for another job.

Speak to someone you trust about what the best steps forward could be.

Remember: your safety is the most important thing. If you are feeling threatened or unsafe then it's not a good idea to answer back or stand up to the person who is bullying you. If you're not sure if talking back to them might put you at risk, speak to someone you trust to find out what they think.

Cyberbullying and trolls

Cyberbullying is the same as bullying, only it is bullying that happens online. It can take several different forms:

- Someone you know (from school, work or somewhere else) sending you nasty messages or writing horrible things about you online.
- Someone you don't know (and who only knows of you through social media) sending you nasty messages or writing horrible things about you online.

If you are being cyberbullied by someone from work or from school, you can take similar steps to the ones we looked at around bullying. We'll look at them again, but with an online twist.

If you are active on social media, and talk about being LGBTQIA+ or autistic, there are people out there who might decide to attack you for it. People who comment on your posts or message you just to be nasty are called 'trolls'.

This doesn't mean you should stop talking about these

things. Social media can be an amazing place to talk about important things, explore your identity and find people who have similar experiences. But there are steps you can take to stop the trolls from hurting you.

Blocking and ignoring it

Many bullies do horrible things in order to get a reaction, so sometimes ignoring them can be the best way to make them stop. You won't necessarily know if this is true for your bully until you try it.

If someone calls you a name, or makes fun of you, or is nasty to you online, most social media platforms give you the option to block or unfriend them. This will mean that they can't see or comment on your posts, and you can't see theirs.

Sometimes, when you block someone, they may still be spreading nasty messages about you to people you know. At this point, you may have to ask the people you know on the social media platforms to also block the person. If you know that they are still saying nasty things about you online, even if you can't see it, this can still hurt.

If you are unable to ignore it, but don't want to publicly react to it, it might be useful to talk about it with someone you trust, either in person, through text or online. Let yourself cry about it and shout about it with someone you feel safe with.

As with bullying, if someone is causing you real harm through cyberbullying – triggering your dysphoria, damaging your mental health or threatening to hurt you – then it might not be a good idea to try to ignore it. For your own safety and wellbeing, it's important that you speak out.

Reporting them and speaking out

If someone is continuing to harass you or spread nasty messages about you, even if you have blocked by them on social media, you might want to think about reporting them for harassment.

Most social media platforms have ways to report individual posts, tweets or accounts. If they are harassing you by using slurs or saying insulting things about you being autistic or being LGBTQIA+, there are ways to report them for attacking 'protected characteristics'. The social media platform will then look at the post, tweet or account, and see whether they have done enough to have their posts, tweets or accounts deleted.

However, social media platforms are notoriously inconsistent when it comes to upholding complaints about people's behaviour. In these cases, you might want to consider locking your account or making it private (meaning that only people who already follow you or are friends with you can interact with your posts and tweets) until it eases up.

Sometimes, the people being mean to you online might be people you know in real life.

If you know them from school, you might want to get in touch with a teacher, a teaching assistant, or your parent or guardian. You, or someone you trust, may want to email someone to let them know that something is going on. Make sure that you take some screenshots of what the person is saying, as proof of what has been going on.

If you know them from work, you might want to get in touch with a colleague, your manager, another manager that you trust, or go straight to someone in your company's Human Resources team. Like with school, you, or someone you trust, may want to email one of these people to let them know what's going on. Again, make sure that you take some screenshots of what the person is saying, as proof of what has been going on.

However, if you do speak out, there is not always a guarantee that the situation will be dealt with. This doesn't mean that you shouldn't speak out. But you need to be aware that, sometimes, people with the power to help you might not help you.

Some people in power (teachers, managers, parents) can also be bullies. They might even be the ones who are bullying you – or they might not be willing to help you. You are not alone if this is the case.

If you speak out, and the people you speak out to don't help you, you might want to look at getting away from the situation. If you are in school, this might mean speaking to someone you trust (such as your parent or guardian) about moving schools. If you are at work, this might mean looking for another job.

Speak to someone you trust about what the best steps forward could be.

If you block someone on social media, there is always a chance that they might create a new account and begin to be nasty again. In this case, continue to block and report them as soon as they pop up again.

Remember: if you receive abuse or harassment online, don't be afraid to make your account private or locked, or to block as many people as you like. I have found that blocking nasty people, rather than trying to argue with them to 'change their mind' (they very rarely want to have their minds changed) is a much better way of dealing with it and making sure that my mental health is okay.

Bigotry and injustice

Even if you don't receive abuse directly, seeing the things that are thrown at other people can be really difficult. Contrary to popular belief, autistic people often do feel a lot of empathy (we just don't always show it in the way that non-autistic people expect us to).

With a 24-hour news cycle, and many autistic people relying on social media for socializing with their friends and community, bad news has become harder to avoid. It's a particular struggle when we see injustice and bigotry aimed at our communities.

You might see and struggle with:

- people being abused for their sexuality or gender
- people being abused for their autism
- people (particularly celebrities or other influential people) spreading bigotry about sexuality, gender, or autism
- reports of hate crimes
- reports of laws across the world that impact LGBTQIA+ and autistic people.

For many of us, simply logging off from social media is not an option. This would mean cutting ourselves off from our community and friends and ignoring our need to be aware of the things that are happening in the world.

However, here are some things that you can do to take care of yourself – because *you* are important.

Schedule in time away from social media/news
This doesn't mean logging off from social media for days at

a time. Just pop some time in your routine every day to do something else that brings you joy.

Whether it's watching a film or a TV show, reading or writing, doing puzzles, playing video games, or something else that makes you smile or keeps you engaged, do what you need to do. It's often easier to properly turn off your social media if you find something else to fill the time.

This is particularly useful before bed, to make sure you're not swept up in all of those intense feelings just before trying to sleep.

Talk about it with someone you trust
Whether it's a parent, a guardian, a friend, or a therapist, talking about the intense feelings you are having can help you to sort through them.

If you can't put it into words, or if you are non-speaking, there are other things you can do. This includes:

- writing letters
- texting
- private or direct messaging
- online chat services (there are online chats where you can speak anonymously to trained people).

You can also write it down just for yourself. Keeping a journal can be a really helpful way of doing things.

Block and report bad people
If there are celebrities who are saying bigoted things about your community, it's best not to try to argue with them or their followers.

I tried to make a celebrity 'see sense' once, and they

ended up retweeting my tweets with nasty comments to their millions of followers. This can incite a 'pile on', where they deliberately expose you to their followers in order to get them to attack you.

Even if you don't follow a toxic person, there's always a chance that they could make their way onto your social media feed. If someone's tweets are upsetting you, you can mute or block them to stop yourself from having to see them. It also doesn't bring attention to them for saying a terrible thing (as we said, some bullies thrive on attention).

The same applies to people who aren't celebrities, but are just being nasty on social media.

As discussed with bullying, you can also report tweets or accounts that are being bigoted. Social media platforms don't always pay attention, but there's no harm in trying.

Mute certain words
Twitter gives you the option of muting certain words or phrases. If certain slurs about your sexuality, gender or autism are particularly triggering for you, you can set your Twitter so that you don't see those words at all. This can make your feed a lot safer for you. If you're feeling stronger later on, you can unmute these words.

Lots of people will put a 'trigger warning' or a 'content warning' on their tweets or social media posts if they are going to talk about a certain subject. You can mute these too (e.g. someone may not be saying a slur against disabled people, but they might be talking about the word so may tag it 'ableist slurs').

Make sure you also tag warnings if you are talking about something sensitive or upsetting. The best way to do this is to start the tweet with 'tw' (trigger warning) or 'cw' (content warning), a colon (:) and then the thing that you are warning about. You can reach out to people about what sorts of warnings are helpful to you, and let other people know that they can approach you with the same information.

Focus on things you can do

If you are feeling overwhelmed by the amount of things that are awful in the world, zero in your focus on what you *can* do, rather than feeling helpless.

- Is there a petition to sign?
- Is there a fund or organization you can donate to?
- Is there a politician you can write to?
- Are there things you can write about it?
- Are there books you can read about it?
- Is there art you can make to raise awareness of it?
- Is there someone you know who you can educate about it?
- Is there a protest you can sign up to (many protests may also have virtual versions, so if you can't make it to the actual protest, there may be an online option for attending)?

Doing something and then passing it on to other people can be a *big* way to get rid of those feelings of powerlessness and can focus all that emotional energy into something constructive. Not only does it help you, but it also helps you fight back against some of the bad stuff in the world.

Fighting back

This is the last thing we are going to be talking about in this book. And, because of that, it's going to be positive.

Always remember that you are not helpless. You do not have to just watch bad things, bigotry and injustice in the world. There are ways that you can fight back. There are ways that you can try to make the world a better place for you and other people in your community.

Set up a platform for yourself
If you care a lot about an issue and you want to be heard, the best thing to do is to create a platform for yourself. Social media can be a fantastic place for this. You can set up a Twitter account or a Facebook page focused entirely around the things that you are passionate about and the stories you want to tell.

If you have lots to say, you can start a blog! This is a great way to get out some of those feelings, and potentially help other people as well. Sites like Wordpress and Tumblr can help you set up a blog for free, but may have additional content you can pay for if your blog starts to take off. You can also share your blog on your social media platforms. This is a great way to find your voice and get people listening to what you want to say.

I started my blog several years ago, as a way to try to make a difference, to get out my anger and also to tell my story. From there, I have been able to actually speak publicly about my experiences as a queer autistic woman, have discovered a community online, have made a difference in at least one person's life, and am now writing a book!

If you feel up to it, you could even start a YouTube channel or a podcast! If you have a phone with a camera or a voice recorder, you can get started. There is no need for fancy equipment – if you become more successful, then you can think about investing further.

Building a platform for yourself can be a long process. It can build up one person at a time. You might not get the audience that you thought you might. And you will always be learning new things and changing your views as you talk about things with other people. You will probably get things wrong. For example, if you are white, you are talking about things from a white perspective – if a person of colour calls you out, and says that something you've done is racist or just incorrect, don't get defensive. Listen, learn, apologize, and do better next time.

If you gain a platform, then you have a responsibility for the things you say. Think about that before considering if you want one or not.

Set up a group
If you're in school, you can look into setting up an LGBTQIA+ group. In some places, this is called a 'Gay Straight Alliance', where LGBTQIA+ students and supportive (even curious) non-LGBTQIA+ allies are encouraged to spend time together, talk and campaign for changes in the school environment. Encouraging non-LGBTQIA+ allies, and advertising it as such, can also make it safer for people who are currently closeted to attend without fear of being outed.

When I was at secondary school, my school was not welcoming to LGBTQIA+ students; it wasn't talked about, girls were told off for linking arms, and a teacher was told she wasn't allowed to recommend material to me on being LGBTQIA+ when she suspected some of my (many) issues were related to my sexuality (she was correct!). But now, ten years after I left? Due to the work of students in setting up a group like this, they are considered one of the most LGBTQIA+ friendly schools in the country!

Of course, it's not just schools where this can work. If you work and you join a union, many unions have LGBTQIA+ and disability-specific groups that you can join. They will often meet, talk about and campaign on issues of discrimination in the workplace. Sectors or individual workplaces may also have LGBTQIA+ or disability groups – and, if they don't, you might want to speak to your manager or Human Resources about setting one up.

Outside school and the workplace, you might want to set up a local group. You can find more information about this in the 'Out and About' chapter.

Resist!
This is the main driving force behind everything I do. Resisting a world that doesn't accept me by accepting myself. Resisting a world that isn't fair by forcing it to be fairer. Resisting a world that doesn't work by being a part of the movement to make it work.

There are lots of different ways you can do activism work. With the advent of the internet, it's constantly evolving. You can be an activist just on social media, or you can be out there, organizing and marching in the streets. The revolution will be accessible for us all.

There may be a local organizing group near you, or you may find one online. Most organizing groups work around a specific type of injustice or bigotry – for example, Lesbians and Gays Support the Migrants is a grassroots organization that campaigns and protests around migrants' rights. It will also show solidarity to other causes, boosting them on its social media and talking about them in its activism.

These types of organizations and groups can help you find real, solid, productive things that you can do. One of my friends even chained himself to a plane once and stopped a deportation flight from happening! But you don't have to be that extreme to get involved – your mental health and safety are important, and you can bring about change while also keeping yourself safe.

There will be resources on taking action, ways to make change and how to do it safely at the end of this chapter. You can also use the advice from the 'Out and About' chapter in order to make attending protests a little bit more accessible for you as an autistic person.

Keep an eye on what's going on in the world. Listen to what people are saying they need. Join them, lift up their voices. Lift up your own voice on issues that *you* are passionate about. You can be an important voice in the fight to end bigotry and injustice against LGBTQIA+ and autistic people. You just have to find your niche.

Because if there's one thing autistic people do well, it's passion.

You can harness that. Whether it's writing, tweeting, marching, building a community or making art that makes people sit up and listen, you *can* resist against a world that doesn't feel fair. And you *can* be a part of changing it.

Be proudly autistic.

Be proudly queer.

And be proudly you.

More information

Books

Trans Teen Survival Guide by Owl and Fox Fisher.

LGBTQ: The Survival Guide for Lesbian, Gay, Bisexual, Transgender, and Questioning Teens by Kelly Huegel Madrone

Resist!: How to Be an Activist in the Age of Defiance by Michael Segalov

Links

Gendered Intelligence: http://genderedintelligence.co.uk/projects/kip/bullying

Stonewall: www.stonewall.org.uk/resources-disabled-lgbt-people-and-lgbt-people-accessibility-needs

National Bullying Helpline: www.nationalbullyinghelpline.co.uk

YouTube videos

The Sex Education You Never Had *PRIDE EDITION* by Ellbat: http://bit.do/Sex-Education-You-Never-Had
In this hour-long video, Ellbat (with an appearance by Fox Fisher) answers lots of questions about all things LGBTQIA+, including how to deal with bullying and prejudice. You can find the questions you need answering, and what time they appear in the video, in the description box for easy access to information.

Reasons to Smile Playlist by Thomas Sanders: http://bit.do/Reasons-To-Smile
This is the most important playlist that I have. So I'm giving it to you. This playlist is a part of my post-meltdown and mental health

plan. I have it on alert on my phone to remind me to watch it whenever I'm struggling. It's a brilliant, happy mix of all the good things that are happening in the world: cute pictures and jokes, but also victories for activists, steps forward for LGBTQIA+ rights, and a reminder it's worth it to keep fighting. It's the ultimate self-care *and* the ultimate inspiration. A reminder to never give up and to never stop being you.

Index